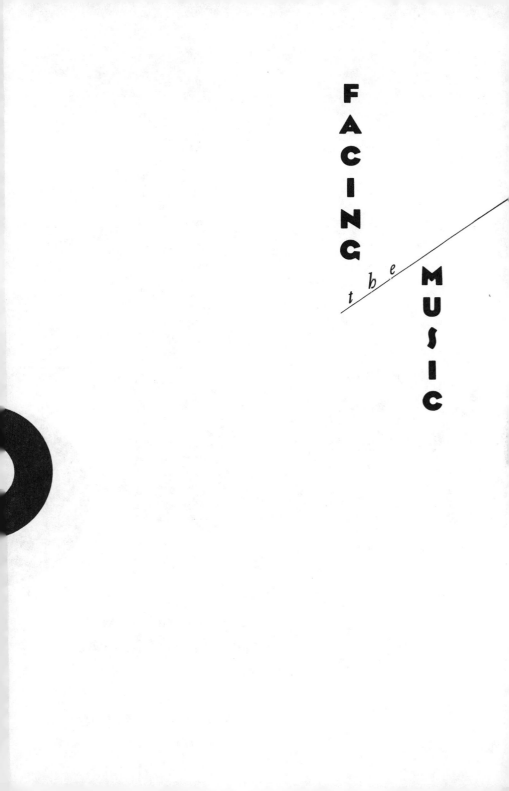

*Other Pantheon guides to popular culture*

**READING THE NEWS**
*Robert Karl Manoff and*
*Michael Schudson, editors*

**WATCHING TELEVISION**
*Todd Gitlin, editor*

# FACING the MUSIC

*A pantheon guide to popular culture*

## SIMON FRITH, EDITOR

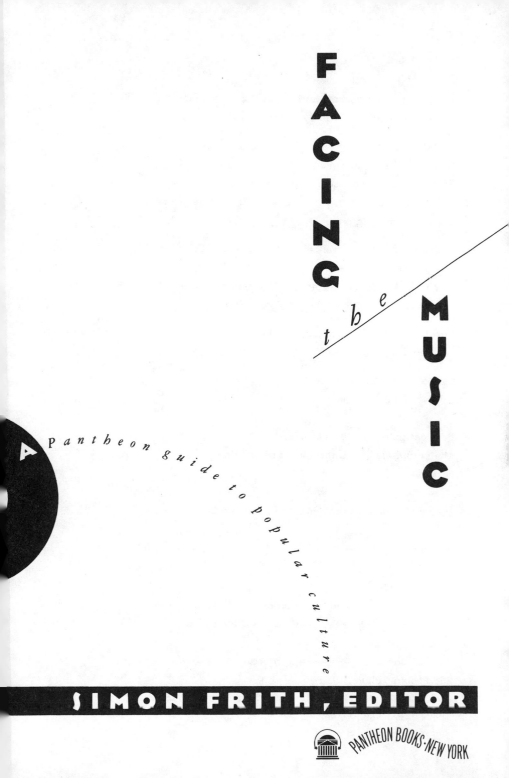

PANTHEON BOOKS·NEW YORK

Book design by Archie Ferguson
Manufactured in the United States of America
First Edition

Library of Congress Cataloging-in-Publication Data

Facing the music.
    Bibliography: p.
    Includes index.
    Contents: Top 40 radio / Ken Barnes—Ain't No Mountain High Enough / Steve Perry—Video pop / Simon Frith—[etc.]
    1. Popular music—History and criticism.
    2. Popular culture.  I. Frith, Simon.
ML3470.F22   1989       784.5'00973        88-42595
ISBN 0-394-55849-9
ISBN 0-394-75185-X (pbk.)

# CONTENTS

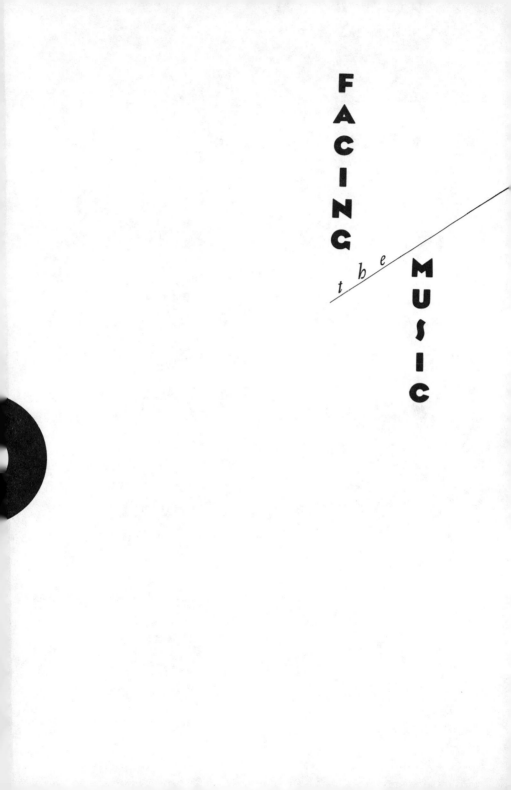

# FACING the MUSIC

# INTRODUCTION

**I**n March 1988 the marketing director of HMV Records (the biggest record-selling retail chain in Britain) told startled delegates at the annual meeting of the British Radio Academy that the single record would be obsolete within three years. T-shirts, he reported, already represented a bigger percentage of HMV's turnover than 45 rpm discs (9 percent to 8 percent) and a much more economical use of display space. Singles, he argued, are only commercially useful these days as a means of promotion (trailing stars, films, and albums), and while this may suit radio programmers and video outlets (in the market for cheap forms of entertainment), it no longer makes economic sense to retailers (or their customers).

In the United States the impact of MTV did boost singles' sales for a while, but only briefly, and there have long been mutters from within the business about the irrationality of organizing the sales process (the charts, the news, the plugs) around the least profitable music product. The odds are that by 1990 the 45 rpm record will have gone the way of the 78, and an era of twentieth-century popular music will be over. For those of us who've measured our emotions in hits, in three- and four-minute stretches of joyful, sorrowful, gleeful voices, marking place and memory, giving us our most intense, most unexpected sense of self, the single—the song that suddenly appears in our lives and shapes them for a moment—defines the *art* of mass music.

This book is about the most sustained example of that art —rock music—and it is inspired by the suspicion (my suspicion, that is) that the rock story is ending. This makes it possible, for the first time, to make sense of it. One of the peculiar characteristics of rock, after all, has been its construction by a variety of commentators—music *watchers*—whose self-appointed task was to interpret sounds, whether as disc jockeys or journalists, moralizers or publicists. The meaning of rock 'n' roll in the 1950s was thus the subject of a running debate between ideological salesmen like Alan Freed and newspapers full of anxious, scoffing, "grown-ups." The subsequent transformation of rock 'n' roll into the teen pop of the late 1950s and early 1960s was orchestrated by Dick Clark on *American Bandstand,* by the pix and trivia of *Sixteen* magazine. The late 1960s interpretation of rock as a serious cultural business was led by writers in *Rolling Stone, Crawdaddy,* and *Creem,* in *Melody Maker* and *New Musical Express.* The punk movement of the 1970s was determined as much by its press and radio ideologues as by the musicians themselves. Even now, in the fragmented 1980s, a rock record is launched with far more commentary (far more *knowing* commentary) than a new film, TV show, or advertisement.

Rock 'n' roll was from the start, then, constituted not simply as music but also as knowledge. To be a rock fan is not just to like something but also to know something, to share a secret with one's fellow fans, to take for granted the ignorance of nonfans. This common sense of rock fandom has had a constricting effect on the development of rock theory: the huge number of words devoted to rock in the consumer press is matched by the few words devoted to it in the intellectual press. In the relentless speculation on mass culture that defines postmodernism, rock remains the least treated cultural form. The common sense of rock, to put this another way, is that its meaning is known thoughtlessly: to understand rock is to *feel* it. Among left-leaning intellectuals the attitude is a generalized disdain for rock's commercialism and vulgarity coupled with a commitment to an individual artist or song or genre. Hype—the driving force of the rock sales process—is taken to be transparent in its motivation and effects; taste, the reason why particular people like particular sounds, is taken to be mysterious, inaccessible to reason. In a world in which everyone is an expert—everyone knows what makes their music significant, other people's music vacuous—self-proclaimed expertise is despised. Rock critics despise rock academics, rock musicians despise rock critics, rock fans despise each other.

This book is written to challenge common sense and should therefore annoy everyone. Mary Harron argues that hype isn't peripheral to good music (as it is usually described) but crucial to its power and pleasures. In her reading, rock ideology is less a counter to pop patter than another (more deluded) version of it. Ken Barnes examines music radio, which continues to be the basic rock institution even if it is largely ignored by rock writers. As he shows, radio's continuous pursuit of "demographics" reflects the basic contradictions of rock as a cultural form: its celebration simultaneously of the novel and the familiar, its definition of collectivity as merely the sum of any number of individual choices. Jon Savage suggests that "youth," rock's core audience (or market), has always been an ideological construct and has always fed off the interpretation of the music as a sexually inflected kind of fun. The changing nature of the youth market (the rock audience) is not just a demographic matter, not just a material effect; it also marks changing fears and fantasies, changing accounts of hetero- and homosexuality, changing anxieties of affluence and lack. Steve Perry describes the musical relationship of blacks and whites in explicitly socialist terms. For him what's at issue in the white exploitation of black music and musicians is not the authenticity of a sound (where it comes from) but its resonance (where it goes). The current commercial success of "crossover" is a sign of opportunities seized, he maintains, not lost. Finally, in my own essay on the industry, I outline the global leisure context in which music is now made. The conventional model of center and periphery on which rock's account of itself as commercially radical depends (the model of heroic independent companies competing with the majors, matching economic muscle with cultural guile) is obsolete. Rock is now the sound of worldwide film and television entertainment: its commercial importance is the most effective way of delivering the right audience to the right advertisers.

None of these essays are objective—though all are, I believe, definitive—and they certainly don't have a shared line. If we do all understand rock culture in terms of struggle, we disagree quite sharply about the present state of that struggle. Jon Savage and I write with a sense that the time when rock could be unsettling is over; we are, for the moment, pessimists. Mary Harron and Ken Barnes write from the assumption that the pop/rock, sales/art dialectic is a built-in feature of all mass music; they are thus cheerful fatalists. Steve Perry hears something empowering in the present confusion of sound and race and class; he is an optimist.

In commissioning these essays I made three requests. First, I asked everyone to write with a sense of history. One of the central tenets of rock common sense (particularly in the United States) is that there is a pure, truthful, rock 'n' roll sound against which all popular music should be measured. Such measurement produces the familiar myths of authenticity and corruption, the rock epic of the rise and fall of stars and styles and subcultures. I asked my writers to bear these myths in mind, to remember that rock values are the residue of more than thirty years of argument. Second, I stressed to my writers that rock is a peculiarly cross-national form; it is an Afro-American music whose biggest or, at least, most ideologically influential stars have been British. (And the Anglo-American connection is reflected here directly: Jon Savage and I are British, Ken Barnes and Steve Perry are American, Mary Harron is a Canadian based in Britain who started her writing career in New York.) Third, while I didn't want any writer to become unduly concerned with definitions of pop and rock, I did want everyone to reflect on the role of labeling in the rock process. Labels (pop and rock, metal and punk, crossover and New Age, etc., etc.) seem to me to offer the best clues to how different musics work in people's lives, and I was curious to see what my essayists would make of this.

In the end, though, the most interesting aspect of these pieces is something else: how surely the writers move from the particular experience of a song or star or video, of a radio or sales campaign, to a general account of how and why rock matters. This is the fan's way of thinking and it is the reverse of orthodox left-wing cultural theory which, following Adorno's example, continues to assess mass culture in general before claiming the glorious exceptions to its rules (Dylan and Lennon, punk, Springsteen, Prince). Our starting point is different. For us, any general theory of mass culture must lie in the immediacy of our everyday pleasure in pop.

# KEN BARNES

# A fragment

# of the

# imagination

**TOP 40 / RADIO**

**Y**ou jump in the car and turn on the radio. Driving along, you ignore the DJ's patter, but the hardsell software spot propels your finger to the pushbutton. New station—another, less obnoxious commercial, then a song—not bad, nothing, really nothing to turn off, but your mind wanders a bit. Then the jolt, the familiar ringing intro of your favorite new song. Right hand lunges for the volume knob, you crank that sucker up, and it's a good thing for your fellow drivers you've got the air conditioning on and the windows up, because you're wailing along with that tune with every decibel your poor ragged voice can summon up.

It's a great feeling. Despite your having already bought the song on album, cassette, and CD, and home-taped it on one of your custom in-car cruise music anthologies, the sensation is not diminished. The shock of sudden recognition, the pleased surprise of hearing your favorite song on the car radio in airsealed intimacy, can't be duplicated. Of course you've tuned into the station in the first place because you have a reasonable expectation it will play your current favorite, but you're never sure exactly *when,* and it's that spontaneous thrill you experience when it actually comes on that you're seeking.

# HIT RADIO:
# THE RATIONALE

**H**it radio is one of America's great cultural inventions. A shining example of the classic free-enterprise, give-the-people-what-they-want commercial device, it revitalized a medium consigned to its deathbed upon the advent of television in the early fifties. It has kept radio healthy through waves of technological epidemics—cable, video games, video recorders, MTV, cassettes and tape decks, CDs—that allow listeners to acquire their favorites in a multitude of configurations.

Consider these hit radio guiding principles:

- The listener wants to hear his favorite numbers again and again.

- The programming of music is controlled entirely by the choice of the public. If the public suddenly showed a preference for Chinese music, we would play it.

- The growing universality of musical taste appears to make possible the application of a single programming standard to many individual markets.

- The disc jockey is not representative of the public. Because he is usually above the audience mentally and financially, and lives with popular music, his own preferences are a dangerous guide.

These guidelines, taken from a 1957 article on Top 40 pioneer Todd Storz,[1] apply remarkably well to hit radio today. But thirty years ago, a broadbased Top 40 format, along with country music and rhythm and blues (R&B) formats playing hits from separate musical universes for specialized audiences, served the needs of the radio audience. Today that audience, spanning the 18- to 49-year-old spectrum coveted by advertisers, has been sliced and diced into dozens of minute demographically, psychographically, and sociologically fine-tuned targets, each served by a specific contemporary radio format.

Radio's history is one of fragmentation. The medium started the way network TV operates now, programming blocs of mostly network-supplied entertainment. Smaller stations employed more local programming, but in either case an impossibly wide diversity was the rule. An opera might lead into a country music show (such a juxtaposition gave the Grand Ole Opry its name); a news discussion would be followed by a polka party, a baseball broadcast (probably re-created via wire-service reports), a live drama, a ventriloquist (a form of entertainment ideally unsuited to radio—how did Edgar Bergen become such a big radio star?), a soap opera, and on into the night.

Television, with visuals that could convey drama and comedy (not to mention ventriloquism) more vividly, paved the way for the first radio revolution. Recorded music, which does not require the attention spoken-word entertainment demands, became radio's key programming element. The objections of the musicians' union, which rightly felt records deprived musicians of on-air work, and record companies, which wrongly believed that if people heard records on the air, they wouldn't want to buy them, had been resolved in the late forties, and the way was clear for a new kind of radio.

The Top 40 approach, devised by Storz in 1953 and adopted by legions of imitators, played the hits of the day in rotations designed to give listeners a very good chance of hearing their favorite song. (As long, that is, as your favorite song was the same as everyone else's, which was likely because Top 40 devotees were hearing the same forty contemporary hits, creating a neat, closed circle effect that works to this day.) Top 40 quickly proved to be the most efficient and audience-attracting method of playing music, and gave radio the form and content that TV couldn't provide.

# READY TO ROCK

When rock 'n' roll developed in the mid-fifties, arising from the R&B and country music heard on specialized stations from the late forties on, it had the perfect medium for exposure already in place. At the same time, Top 40 radio had a style all its own, along with a new, largely untapped audience for it—teenagers.

As advertisers and culture brokers of the fifties discovered in a number of areas, teenagers controlled the leisure-time choices of their entire families. Adults didn't stop listening to ballgames or make-believe ballroom dance music shows, but they deferred to their kids and left the dial on Top 40 stations for lengthy periods. The ratings services of the day (using relatively unsophisticated techniques compared to today's subatomically examined data) showed Top 40 outlets with 40-, 50-, 60-percent shares of the radio audience.

As the teenage population and influence rose in the early sixties, Top 40 increased its dominance. The whopping shares of the first Top 40s were reduced, but only because three or four stations now vied for the market supremacy once owned by a single Top 40.

The late fifties and early sixties became a volatile Top 40 battleground, as stations staged the most outrageous contests, the wildest stunts, hired the most manic DJs, and ran wide-open playlists, hoping to uncover the newest irresistible smash. (The "40" in Top 40 was a guideline rather than a strict playlist limit; stations in the early sixties often played seventy, eighty, or more records, to the detriment of effective music rotation.) The era was the stuff of legend.

## DO THE TIGHTEN UP

**B**ut by the mid-sixties, a further fragmenting appeared feasible. The Drake format—named after programmer Bill Drake, who introduced his approach in Fresno and brought it to national attention at Los Angeles's KHJ in 1965 —narrowed Top 40's focus. It didn't eliminate the manic personalities, but confined them to shorter outbursts. Contests and promotions remained extravagant and were designed for maximum notoriety. But the music was reined in: Drake stations aired a tight thirty-record playlist, plus a few "hitbound" extras.

The Drake format wasn't really a radical reworking so much as a return to the basic Top 40 principles: play the hits over and over. Rotations were refined to feature the "powers," the six or eight hits that the audience wanted to hear most of all. Airplay statistics consistently show the top eight or so records ranking far above the other "hits" of the day in total exposure. Notwithstanding the romantic notion of a "Top 40" or a "Hot 100," the number of *real* hits at any given time is far smaller.

The Drake formula worked. Drake stations and their imitators (who tended to take the format even further into realms of restriction and leached most of the personality from it) scored substantial ratings triumphs. They also paved the way for radio's next revolution, yet a further fragmentation of radio's imagination.

Certain visionaries realized that a significant portion of the radio audience wasn't being served by a constant diet of the hits, that there was now more to the musical universe than the Top 40. Of course that idea was hardly revelatory. Country records rarely had enough widespread appeal to crack Top 40 playlists, but were quite popular in certain areas. (As time and geographical redistribution wore on, the regionalism of the country format became a much less important factor—there are still more country stations in the South, where the music is rooted, but there are few cities anywhere in the nation without a country station.)

Similarly, there were audience clusters who wanted to hear nothing but R&B records, and not just the ones that were acceptable enough to mass audience ears to join the pop records on Top 40. Jazz and classical buffs, too, had stations of their own, although they usually pulled down miniscule ratings.

# TAKING THE LONG-PLAY HOME

**B**y the mid-sixties the first rock 'n' roll schism was underway. A heady climate of musical experimentation, sparked by the Beatles, Rolling Stones, Beach Boys, and other leading hitmakers, turned the album into a playground of innovation, and transformed the roles of the single and LP configurations.

The album had served as an afterthought to the single, being a hastily assembled collection of often second-rate tunes designed to capitalize on the hit single's appeal. Now the LP became a medium for more advanced artistic expression, with singles representing the safer, more conventional creations. In most cases, this made for better theory than practice, but the cultural explosion of 1965–69 produced enough masterworks to establish the mythology of the album as the definitive yardstick of an artist's abilities.

Meanwhile, Top 40 radio was strictly concerned with playing the hit singles and, thanks to the Drake legions, more restrictive than ever. It should be noted, however, that, even if restrictive, Top 40 recognized what sold. If the hits included six-minute Bob Dylan ballads, outspoken political protest songs, and experimental flights of fancy from the Beatles, Stones, Byrds, and Yardbirds, that was what radio played.

However, there was suddenly a quantity of quality rock around and no place to hear the superstar album cuts and tracks by newer innovative artists who hadn't earned their Top 40 hitmaker credentials. By a particularly neat dovetailing of unrelated circumstances, suddenly there was a place to hear it.

Although capability for FM broadcasting had existed for decades, and FM stations were on the air, AM was the band of renown. Most car radios, a key listening outlet (undermined only slightly by the inconvenient eight-track tape player in the sixties and even now relatively unaffected by the convenient cassette deck), were AM-only. All the big Top 40 stations, as well as the news and information outlets and full-service, middle-of-the-road (MOR) giants, were on AM. FM was for foreign-language programming, jazz, and non-profit radio, or, when owned by the proprietor of an AM station, for simulcasts of the AM's format.

The Federal Communications Commission, in an effort to develop the FM band, prohibited stations from simulcasting more than 50 percent of their programming. FM owners had to scramble for something to put on the air. In a few key markets, notably San Francisco and New York, innovative programmers, who'd picked up on the simmering dissatisfaction of many music fans with Top 40, were able to convince FM owners to try a new approach—eclectic, freeform, album rock radio.

The music these stations played wasn't the only thing that was different about them. Sensing a need for complete dissociation from the mechanics and conventions of Top 40, former fast-talkers like Tom Donahue, Murray the K, and Scott Muni mellowed down, adopting conversational on-air approaches closer to the styles of the jazz grotto hipsters on the specialty shows. The freeformers junked Top 40 jingles, threw out the rotation schedules, allowed DJs to pick the music, and scrapped time restrictions so that extended works of art like "The End" by the Doors or "In-A-Gadda-Da-Vida" by Iron Butterfly could be aired in their entirety.

Mellow hipspeak wasn't all freeform rock radio borrowed from jazz. Jazz itself was played in significant amounts (at first), along with the staple rock LP tracks. So was folk music, ragas, spoken word, blues, and a smidgen of soul, until it became clear—around the dawn of the seventies  that the eclectic stuff was more a turnoff than an inducement. The majority of listeners would really rather have heard "White Room" one more time, thanks.

Freeform was more of an aesthetic revolution than a commercial one. It found a hole, an unserved fragment, and met its audience's needs. Very quickly every major city had a freeform rocker, usually two. But the stations rarely if ever rivaled the big Top 40s for overall ratings. The "demographic age" was not yet upon radio. (Ratings were still keyed on a mass audience of 12 years old and over, instead of the more focused age cells of 18 to 24, 25 to 34, and 35 to 49, that would later become much more important.) However, even if demographics had been important, the 18-to-24-year-old male counterculturalites who made up the bulk of freeform's audience would not have been a prime target for advertisers, who favored adult consumers who bought into the (high-ticket) consumer ethic.

# THE BIRTH OF AOR

**R**ock music itself continued to evolve in an album-oriented direction, especially as record companies geared up to maximize the profit potential of the more expensive LP, rather than the single. The 45 was still the prime come-on for the album, the most commercial cut, but labels were aware that exposure for an LP's other tracks could stimulate further sales (and sometimes uncover a future hit single).

Album rock was still an attractive format, but its freedom and resultant excesses hindered its potential for ratings success and its ability to influence record sales. Corrective measures were taken, many pioneered by the ABC radio chain, which made a strong commitment to the album rock format in the early seventies but demanded a more controlled environment.

Control of the music was taken from disc jockeys and returned to program directors, who set guidelines on what to play and when to play it (often with the strong input of national consultants). The fringe elements of the music mix were eliminated, leaving the rock core. Lengthy DJ raps were trimmed, although pains were still taken to sound as countercultural, hip, mellow, and un—Top 40 as possible. The result was hit radio with a different universe of hits.

Only the most stubborn give-me-freeform-or-give-me-death proponents would regard the honing of freeform into album-oriented rock (AOR) as an evil plot against musical freedom. The restrictions did eliminate some groundbreaking, exciting, adventurous radio. They also wiped out mass quantities of self-indulgent, hopelessly excessive, infuriatingly amateurish broadcasting. They gave rock fans consistent presentations and the realistic hope of hearing their favorite songs when they tuned in—the cornerstone of not just Top 40 but American hit radio of any kind. And listeners no longer had to endure a fifteen-minute drum solo to get to their favorites.

With the refinement of AOR, Top 40 faced its first serious competitor. Country stations played a completely different world of hits and had older listeners. R&B stations played a lot of the same music as Top 40 (the latter format airing the R&B hits with the widest appeal), but had a cradle-to-grave, mostly black audience and rarely had the signal strength (or financial resources) to battle on equal terms. Now the AOR stations cut into the Top 40 listener pool with plenty of shared music plus the attraction of greater depth, a cutting-edge image (AOR stations could play a hot track right off the album without having to wait for it to be issued as a single), and the superior FM band to showcase the music.

The last point can't be overemphasized. The most enduring legacy of freeform rock was that FM was where it's at. The attraction of stereo, which had obliterated mono on record in 1967, convinced a generation of listeners that music sounded inferior in AM monaural, a perception that has never been shaken. Today AM is virtually dead as a music medium.

While most AM Top 40s were unable to survive the FM onslaught (WABC in New York has been a talk station for almost a decade now; Los Angeles's KHJ switched to country and then to various oldies presentations), the format itself survived by jumping to FM, as owners with both an FM and AM facility in the same market simply switched their Top 40s to the FM side. But even after band jumping, Top 40 had another flank carved up by the next radio revolution—adult contemporary.

# AC DOES IT

Adult contemporary developed out of the simple recognition that people who were in their thirties and forties by
the mid-seventies had lived with rock 'n' roll for twenty years,
and younger adults essentially knew nothing else. Middle-of-
the-road (MOR) stations that avoided rock were finding their
audiences getting older. More sophisticated ratings services
like Arbitron, which became the industry standard in the seventies, were able to prove how important the aging process
was becoming. Since young adults comprised the bulk of the
consuming population, a graying audience was not a cheering prospect.

At the same time, in reaction to the psychedelic era and the
emergence of hard rock and proto–heavy metal in the early
seventies, a pronounced trend toward singer-songwriters
came to the fore. Artists like Carole King, James Taylor, and
Cat Stevens had enormous Top 40 hits. They combined two
attributes: they attracted young adults who may have been
put off by the children of Cream and Hendrix (Grand Funk,
for instance); and, equally important, didn't offend the anti-
rock older adults.

Soft rock of the singer-songwriter sort enabled stations to
attract advertisers' cream demographic segment: 25-to54-
year-old adults. This audience was more settled and prosper-
ous than the younger, rowdier AOR fans. The AC audience
didn't include the proportionately decreasing teens who still
made up much of Top 40's listenership. It had loads of dispos-
able income.

Combining the softer contemporary hits with the acceptable oldies from the top rock artists (playing "Yesterday" but
passing on "Revolution") proved a remarkably successful format. MOR stations were able to evolve gradually and grace-
fully toward adult contemporary, while other stations
converted to it. By the end of the seventies, AC was the most

popular format in the country (a distinction it still holds), severely cutting into Top 40's sphere of influence.

## DANCIN' FOOLS

**A** final revolution dealt a devastating blow to Top 40 in the seventies: disco. Radio was not terribly quick to capitalize on the dancing-in-clubs phenomenon that swept the country beginning about 1973 and blossomed about five years later. The principal radio beneficiaries were the stations aiming at black audiences. Most of the music popular in discos was by black artists, and disco hits peppered the R&B charts, coexisting comfortably with ballads and funk. Stations like WBLS in New York kept their ears to the clubs and scored big ratings successes. Other stations added disco segments at night, and eventually WKYS in Washington, D.C., WKTU in New York, and a few others tried disco as a full-scale format, with simply fabulous results—at first.

Where was Top 40 when the dance craze was fermenting? Right where it always was, picking off the disco hits with the greatest mass appeal ("The Hustle," "Get Down Tonight") to add to its variety-pack music mix. Top 40 can be termed a "vulture" format, preying on other formats to pounce on their best and brightest hits. A Top 40 playlist is characteristically made up of rockers, a few ballads, some straight pop, dance-funk stylings, and (until the eighties) a bit of country. Variety has always been Top 40's musical selling point, and it's a formidable position to own, offering the largest potential audience a blend of the best from every format, skillfully deployed so no one gets tired of hearing the same type of song. Listeners, the credo holds, are always willing to stick around through a song they're not crazy about in hopes that the next one will knock their socks off.

But by the turn of the eighties, the vulture seemed vulnerable to being knocked off its perch. AOR had captured many of its teens and young adults (principally males). Disco and its more enduring successor, urban contemporary (slightly broader music base, less pejorative name), were slicing off an entirely different socioeconomic segment (a lot of women, and black and latino young adults). AC was lopping off Top 40's upper end (adults over 25, especially those over 35, with a preponderance of women). Fragmentation prevailed.

# RETREAT TO TIMIDITY

Top 40 did not help its own cause much. It ran scared, mostly in fear of AC, allowing urban and more traditional black stations on one side, and AORs on the other, to take the new music initiative. Top 40 appeared conservative by comparison, playing the vulture role to the extreme and picking up on other formats' hits late in their life cycles. Meanwhile, AC, even more restrictive in its music selection, was playing the conservative role more successfully.

As competition for ratings points (advertisers' dollars) became hotter, Top 40 overemphasized one of its guiding principles to the detriment of other, equally important, rules. One of the unquestioned maxims of Top 40 programming is *what you don't play can't hurt you*. Avoid at all costs the possibility of playing a record the listener doesn't like. If he can tolerate it, fine, but anything that polarizes listener attitudes is probably better off skipped.

Carried to an extreme, this philosophy leads to rigor mortis. If there's a shadow of a doubt about a record's mass appeal, the tendency is to pass. The records a programmer in that state of mind *can* feel safe in playing are very few, and playlists are accordingly reduced to twenty or fewer songs. This approach works for ACs, which provide a balance and sufficient variety by leaning heavily on proven oldies. But for the more active, younger Top 40 audience, raised on novelty and looking to the Top 40 stations for current hits, a tight playlist, with the consequent increase in rotations on the safest hits, leads to boredom and burnout.

# PASSIVE INSISTENCE

Top 40 exacerbated this prevailing attitude by going research-crazy. Beset on all sides by competition, stations looked for new ways to make sure they were playing the right records and avoiding audience turnoffs. Consultants who specialized in music testing became fashionable, many stressing the "active/passive" nature of the radio audience.

Actives were the people Top 40s had traditionally considered their audience: music fans who followed their favorite artists faithfully, bought records, called in requests, cared about music. Passives enjoyed music, but as a background element. They rarely knew or cared who was singing, seldom bought records, didn't go to concerts. Music was not an obsession with them; it wasn't even particularly important in their lives.

It was pointed out that there are far more passives than actives listening to the radio (incontestably true). Duly admonished, Top 40 programmers looked for ways to test the musical preferences of passives. They couldn't measure record sales or requests, the traditional methods of tracking the pulse of the audience, because passives didn't participate in those activities.

So phone research ("callouts") became the rage. Subjects were phoned at random and played excerpts (usually the chorus, or the song's most prominent "hook") of records down the phone line and asked their opinions. It was a neat research technique (it works admirably in testing burnout on familiar hits), but it ignored the high probability that the Beatles themselves would test lousy down the phone if the listener had never heard them before. Virtually anything unfamiliar will elicit a guarded reaction at best, while familiar material has a much better chance of favorable response, even if it's simply the relief of recognition.

# BLAME IT ON
# THE NOMENCLATURE

All of these developments led to a mossbound philosophy and drained much of the excitement from Top 40 radio. Even the name of the format became an albatross. Ad agencies considered Top 40 a teenager's format, best suited to selling pimple cream. Radio managers, aware of Top 40's shopworn image, which contrasted with its increased adult appeal (teens were going elsewhere—to AOR, urban), thought changing the name would help solve the problem. Thus contemporary hit radio (CHR), actually a more accurate if less history-steeped term, was born.

Surprisingly, CHR made a comeback, flying in the face of the fragmentation phalanx. Although an attitude adjustment on the part of the format played an important part, problems for its competitors were big factors.

The ACs began leaning more heavily on oldies, playing it ultrasafe on new material and becoming ever more conservative in a, perhaps, premature anticipation of the population's aging. In effect, they removed themselves as possible competition for CHR in the current music sweepstakes, and found the upper-demographics battleground they'd dominated suddenly overcrowded with big band stations, nostalgia (pre-rock) formats, and myriad variations of AC. Nowhere is there more fragmentation today than in AC, and stations are now forced to fight among themselves rather than raid CHR's audience.

AOR became a prisoner of its own core audience. Its 18-to-24-year-old males maintained such a narrow definition of acceptable rock that stations courting the more desirable over-25 demographics, or even trying to attract a few females, ran a serious risk of blowing off the listener base. So the range of playable AOR music was not widened, and stations compensated by airing more and more "classics," losing much of their prominence as current music breakers.

Record companies also played a part in the narrowing of AOR. Finding the format a useful promotion vehicle, they stepped up their efforts to orchestrate airplay, releasing "emphasis tracks" on twelve-inch promotional discs and campaigning energetically to convince all stations to play the same track at the same time to provide a sales boost for the LP. Lazy or agreeable programmers acceded, and AOR became a follower format, surrendering its historical mandate to experiment with multiple tracks and find new hits. Combined with the oldies boom (more about that later), this circumstance paved the way for CHR to become the rock hitmaker format.

## DISCO REDUX

**D**isco became such a dirty word by 1981 that the format was declared dead, but it wasn't. It just went underground and reemerged as urban contemporary. Urbans, unlike their more traditional R&B counterparts, weren't hesitant to play a record by a pop artist if the sound was compatible. Their emphasis on upbeat, danceable music won them a wide and diverse new audience. But, thanks largely to advertiser reluctance to buy a format appealing primarily to "ethnics," they suffered economically, and could not muster the resources necessary to fight the CHRs on the promotional front. Advertiser discrimination also influenced many stations to abandon the UC format, often moving to CHR or AC as a safer alternative.

Competitors' hard times aside, CHR deserves a lot of credit for turning itself around. Programmers realized that the passive emphasis had gone about as far as it could, and that there was a gaping hole for new music excitement on the radio. The substantial success of the urban contemporaries was a jolt. So was the quick acceptance of MTV, which was forced by lack of available video product upon its 1981 inception to expose plenty of new, primarily British music, and gained much positive press and record company attention from this happenstance.

CHR, looking for new hits to play, found a compatible partner in MTV, while AOR, the format MTV most closely tried to mirror (in its emphasis on rock and de-emphasis on black music), raised listener hackles when it tried to play the Duran Durans and Eurythmics that MTV banged incessantly, and had to retreat to the safety of the rock mainstream.

The vulture format soared to a new peak in 1983–85, appropriating the urban hits fast enough to nullify much of the UC stations' impact, breaking the new synth-poppers in tandem with MTV, picking a few hit tracks from the AOR lists, generally steering clear of ballads, and downplaying conventional pop material. Oldies were virtually eliminated, and even recurrents—the hits of the past several months that were still played lightly for familiarity's sake—were cut back.

Listeners returned to CHR in droves. New CHRs sprang up everywhere to fight for a piece of the action. Record companies loved it, new music was happening in a big way. Disc jockey personality—which had withered into liner-card-reading robotics during the format's retreat into passivity—returned in the wake of John Lander and Scott Shannon's "Morning Zoo" concept, a chaotic assemblage of wacky characters and instant satire that Shannon propelled to prominence in New York with his instantly successful new CHR, WHTZ (Z100).

In retrospect, 1983–85 will probably go down as a new golden age of hit radio. CHR bucked the tide of narrow casting and almost became the format of universal appeal again. But today it appears that fragmentation has regained the momentum. Mainstream CHRs have been contaminated by the oldies boom of the mid-eighties, and have been narrowing their play lists for positioning purposes, emphasizing rock and cutting down on urban crossovers, or the reverse. Hybrid formats, especially in the volatile, high-stakes no-man's-land between urban and CHR, are threatening CHR's dominance. Some of the hybrids, along with certain urbans, are winning the ratings battles in major markets. The broad-based hit radio format may be in trouble.

For a better understanding of today's radio maze, let's look at the bewildering present-day format array and the reasons radio adopts formats in the first place.

# A GUIDE TO FRAGMENTED FORMATS

I've been bandying about the concept of fragmentation for five thousand words or so, in addition to slinging around a lot of format terminology, without pausing more than briefly for definitions. It's difficult to develop a clear picture of radio in America, much less compare it to the relatively simplistic medium of TV, without a closer look at the present field of formats. The hairsplitting technical jargon is boggling in itself, while the sheer number of miniscule format variations is quite daunting. But radio, with ten thousand commercial outlets, was the first mass medium to face the reality of America's cultural segmentation, and it's a bellwether of the future of American culture as a whole. A no doubt incomplete guide to formats follows.

**ADULT CONTEMPORARY** should be pretty clear from previous context, I hope. It aims for the 25-to-54-year-old age group, advertisers'—and thus radio's—most desired demographic, by playing the less abrasive contemporary hits. This means no hard rock, no heavy funk crossovers, few raucous, upbeat dance tunes (although strident guitar solos and prominent percussion have so infiltrated the contemporary music milieu that they're no stranger to AC airwaves). It also means no pre-rock, no supper club singers, none of the MOR staples of the previous generation. Presentations are adult in tone, no screamers, morning zoos, or party-till-you-pukers holding, down DJ slots, although there's plenty of room for humor (much of it double entendre).

I said earlier that fragmentation has fragged AC more severely than any other format. With the largest audience and dense competition, there's a lot of room to maneuver. There are at least five main subspecies:

- Full-service stations, descendants of the huge MOR mainstays of the forties, fifties, and sixties, play contemporary soft hits but place more emphasis on news, talk shows, community interaction, information, and sports. Personality counts heavily, and full-service is the last consistent bastion of music radio success on AM.

- Gold-intensive radio is built around old songs. Although the entire AC format is substantially oldies-based, 80 to 90 percent of the music heard on GI stations is old. Consequently, their current playlists are tiny (as low as eight records), and they play only the safest AC hits, often waiting until they're going down (or off) the national charts. Their oldies are also the safest of superhits, tested and retested through callouts and auditorium tests (some of which wire participants to measure galvanic responses to records) so they will not offend the casual listener. To the active listener, this format variation sounds incredibly boring, but it offers security and comfort, and many GI stations are among the country's most successful.

• Lite is a generic catchall encompassing everything from the love songs format to easy listening stations (see below) that add vocals to grab a chunk of the lucrative AC audience. Lite stations are more careful about the rockier AC hits, restricting their playlists by sound and often (in the case of love songs stations) subject matter—if it's not romantic, forget it. These stations aim for the upper end of the AC age bracket.

• Music-intensive, the mainstream AC approach, makes music the most important element, and current playlists offer about twenty to thirty records, occasionally more. They're the most aggressive about playing new artists and accept the widest range of crossovers from other formats. For obvious reasons the favored AC variation among record labels, they often lose out to full-service outlets because of a lack of heritage, personality, and nonmusical services; and to gold-intensives or lites because their music isn't as familiar and soothing. However, the best of them are extremely successful (KFMB-FM in San Diego, for example, usually cleans its CHR competition's clock).

• Adult alternative stations feature an AC base and adult presentations with a strong emphasis on other forms of music. These can include jazz, soft-rock LP tracks, or even country, and also the recent phenomenon of quiet storm stations (see heading below), essentially black ACs, and the brand-new breed of New Age stations (see heading below). Expect more variations and many more stations switching to AA approaches in the near future, as fragmentation further divides and conquers.

**AOR** (album-oriented rock) grew out of progressive rock radio, which grew out of freeform, as detailed earlier. In the early and mid-seventies, its musical scope was broader, but nowadays it seldom strays from (white) rock.

While other music formats played singles only, early AOR stations played up to half a dozen tracks off an album during the same period of time. Today it is a rare LP that earns significant airplay on more than one track during any given two-month period. TOR (track-oriented rock) would be a more appropriate name for the format today.

As adults became more important to radio, AOR stations found themselves in a trick bag, as mentioned earlier. Their main demographic cell, men between 18 and 24, was considered relatively undesirable compared to the plum over-25 demos. The format then launched a concerted effort to capture listeners over 25. A few tried softening their music; for the most part this approach resulted in lower overall ratings. More stations stepped up their oldies content, up to 70 percent or more. (Still others converted to AOR oldies as a fulltime format: see classic rock under the gold heading.) AOR's importance as a current music format has lately been questioned as a result of its high gold content. A record in heavy rotation at a CHR station is aired about once every two-and-a-half hours; at AOR, maybe three times a day is the norm.

Subdivisions of AOR, apart from classic rock, are many. The soft rockers still exist in some markets, and may be a miniwave of the future. Closely related are "eclectic" AORs that add jazz and soft rock to the normal rock fare. At the other extreme are hard rock stations, which specialize in heavy metal and other bonecrushing styles, and attract fiercely loyal listeners (and small total numbers). And there are a few commercial modern rock stations, playing what used to be called new wave pop and rock, that are now considered as just another subset of the rock mainstream.

The last remnants of AOR's freeform roots are the dozens of noncommercial college stations that comb the fringes of contemporary music to find the most adventurous new sounds as yet uncoopted by the mainstream stations. Freeform's worst excesses are perpetuated on college radio (often more jarringly owing to the amateur status of the air personalities) and the stations' audiences are very small. Still, these outlets have carved out a niche for themselves as a haven for listeners who can't abide commercial radio and as a minor league system for record companies to test some of their newer, more avant-garde releases in competition with records issued by small independent labels. The college radio arena is, especially with AOR's widespread abdication of its discovery role, increasingly important in the exposure of new music.

AOR on-air presentations still try to preserve the "rock 'n' roll outlaw" attitude of the format's early years, even though the music is safe and predictable. Morning zoos and wake-up crews abound in AOR, with wild and crazy guys perpetrating party animal stereotypes. Some modifications have transpired as the push for older listeners intensifies, but not a great deal —adult rock 'n' rollers, the theory goes, still get a kick out of hedonistic, iconoclastic DJs. After all, you're never too old to rock and roll.

**BEAUTIFUL MUSIC** is scorned as "elevator music" by many, and has become a negative in the advertising community because of old-skewing demos. Muzak-style instrumental versions of popular hits still dominate the format. But many stations now call themselves easy listening, and some are adding soft vocal records and DJs with personality in an attempt to keep up with the times and keep down their audience age.

**BIG BAND** is a self-descriptive format, part of a minor stampede in the late seventies and early eighties, when a few smart radio operators realized that listeners of the pre-rock generation survived in large numbers. These listeners had large proportions of spendable income, but were getting no attention whatsoever outside of beautiful music. Big band stations, many on AM, tended to flash up fairly spectacularly upon their introduction, then settled to relatively low, though generally profitable, levels.

**CHR** has already been covered in depth. Because it is a broad-based format, borrowing music from other contemporary formats, it does not have specific subformats of its own. Instead, stations lean toward certain styles of music. There are stations playing practically no black artists and whose entire playlists are still made up of records among the top seventy-five CHR hits. Other stations stay away from most rock records, compensating with emphasis on urban or AC, again falling squarely within CHR's broad boundaries. A handful stress modern rock. And in Houston there's even a station, KQQK, that plays the CHR hits with Spanish-speaking jocks, newspeople, public service announcements, etc.

CHR stations have retreated from their recent no-oldies hard-line stance in the past couple of years. They now play healthy amounts of recurrents along with some oldies, seldom more than five years old.

**CLASSICAL** radio has a long and lucrative history in major markets with sufficient population to support such a minority-appeal approach. Classical listeners may be few (although occasionally massing enough to register fairly sizable Arbitron shares, notably in Denver), but their economic standing is an ad agency's dream. Skillful classical operators can have it both ways: they've got other owners raising eyebrows at their high profit margins and newspaper radio critics praising highbrows for providing lofty culture over the airwaves.

**COMEDY** formats have been attempted at various junctures, most recently in Washington, D.C., and suburban Los Angeles. They've never prospered. A constant comedy diet doesn't seem to have the appeal of comedy bits interspersed with other programming elements.

**CONTEMPORARY CHRISTIAN RADIO** (CCR) is a relatively recent development arising from a growing Christian music industry that needed a radio outlet for its product. Some stations strive to be indistinguishable from ACs in everything but music content (as consultant Brad Burkhardt has said, "Christians need traffic reports too"[2]), while others maintain a more overtly religious atmosphere. CCR, as it's starting to be known, has its own subdivisions: the AC-styled majority and a few harder-rocking CHR-inspired outlets.

**COUNTRY** is one of the oldest formats, and in total number of stations is the largest (though AC has the most listeners). Many past stereotypes and truisms regarding the format—its strong loyalty to artists rather than to the strength of the latest record, its cornpone presentations and hick audiences—have gone by the board with modernization. Most country stations wouldn't know what to do with an Ernest Tubb record if they could find one in their library. Country is a heavily oldies-based format, up to 70 percent, but oldies rarely reach back before 1970.

In avid country markets there is sometimes room for format gradations, usually along the lines of traditional (older gold, a rootsier sound, often appearing on AM) and modern (fewer oldies, more rock and AC-oriented, present-day country records). The main division between country stations, however, is presentational: the continuous country approach, with never fewer than three records in a row and relatively robot-like personalities, versus the more personality-oriented stations, which seem to be slightly in the ascendancy at the moment.

Country music has livened up to the point that an all-current, upbeat country format variant would be an aesthetic delight. But the country audience isn't large enough to justify the experiment. The format needs to attract younger listeners more open to new sounds, certainly; country audiences, although cosmopolitan and upscale to a degree surprising to many observers (including a lot of ad agencies), still tend to be over 35. So stations feel they have to play it fairly conservatively or risk losing the older core audience while trying to appeal to younger types. They therefore concentrate on familiar music, along the lines of AC's philosophies, which makes it difficult for new music to break through and has led to stagnation in the country music industry. There are currently hopeful signs, with labels aggressively pursuing new acts and radio audiences apparently accepting them in higher-than-usual numbers, but the overall outlook is still a bit bleak.

The situation is not helped by the near-total freeze-out of country crossovers by other formats since 1983, after the "urban cowboy" boom played itself out. There is almost no way for young listeners to become attracted to country unless they stumble onto a country station and stick around long enough to hear something they like; they can't hear the music anywhere else.

**EASY LISTENING RADIO** (ELR) is an umbrella term encompassing beautiful music, big band, nostalgia, "Music of Your Life," and other formats concentrating on nonrock material. Of late some easy listening stations have begun to infringe on AC's upper borders, and artists like Barry Manilow may now be more the preserve of ELR stations than adult contemporaries.

Signs of the times: One of Los Angeles's two easy listening outlets recently converted to an all-vocal format it considers "upper-demo AC," while the other is labeling itself IAC, or instrumental adult contemporary. Though the easy listening format's ratings are often excellent, it means older audience

(45-plus) to ad agencies, and the big bucks are being diverted elsewhere.

**FOREIGN-LANGUAGE** stations air programming for specific ethnic audiences (Hispanic, which is widespread enough to merit its own designation, is not included). Often these stations will mix programs in various unrelated languages, selling time to individual program producers. Foreign-language stations, with extremely specialized appeal, seldom show up in the ratings.

**GOLD** is the blanket term for formats playing exclusively, for all practical purposes, rock 'n' roll era (post-1955) hits of the past. Rock stations have played some oldies for almost as long as there have been oldies to play, but Top 40 has always been a current-driven format. Therefore, the niche for stations catering to listeners' rose-colored memories was available by the mid-to-late sixties, and all-oldies formats have existed for almost twenty years (WCBS-FM in New York being a pioneer). They've survived in the face of strong competition from the near-identical gold-intensive ACs, mostly by delving deeper into their libraries and playing lesser-known and harder-edged hits.

Local variations are everywhere: New York stations play more fifties vocal group records, Los Angeles outlets feature the surf sound more heavily, and smart gold stations research their markets for the hits that may not have happened nationally but scored big on their local Top 40 outlets at the time of their release.

In the last couple of years, a second gold rush has materialized (the first came in the wake of *American Graffiti,* in the mid-seventies), and the format is flourishing in greater diversity than ever before. Besides the mainstream gold outlets, playing CHR hits more or less as far back as 1964 and the British invasion, there are "dawn of rock" stations that play pre 1964 or 1955–65 hits, a handful of country gold stations, and, at last, a few R&B gold outlets, most using a syndicated format called "Heart 'N' Soul."

But the the biggest phenomenon in the world of oldies is "classic rock," which plays AOR hits (meaning, essentially, white rock only) roughly extending from the Beatles to the end of the seventies but concentrating on the 1967–75 heyday of progressive rock (loads of Cream, Doors, Zeppelin, Yes, Creedence, Who, and so on).

Classic rock stations had immediate impact, often unseating long-dominant conventional AORs within one or two ratings books. In reaction, AORs beefed up their own oldies content, with some becoming nearly indistinguishable from classic rock outlets.

**GOSPEL** radio is divided into white gospel and black gospel stations, both varieties concentrated mainly in the South and serving constituencies too small to register in the ratings. Many Southern black music stations (as well as a healthy number in other areas) feature gospel hours and special shows as supplemental programming.

**HISPANIC** radio is bound to increase in importance as the nation's Hispanic population rises. Already in HDHAs (ratings jargon for "high density Hispanic areas") there are stations specializing in both modern and traditional Latin music forms, salsa and mariachi and other regional variations, plus full-service and Spanish-language talk outlets. There's always a Hispanic station or two in Miami's top five listings, and in Los Angeles, San Antonio, and other Southwestern markets they are achieving notable success. One intriguing future format possibility: bilingual English-Spanish contemporary hits.

**JAZZ** is rarely found as a fulltime format on commercial stations, owing to its specialized appeal. It is similar to classical in its ability to attract upscale, loyal listeners, but does not have the same prestigious image. It may also face a commercial threat in the near future from New Age stations, which provide more simpatico mood music for today's 25-to-49-year-old crowd.

The format's cohesion is also menaced by ideological arguments about the relative worth of mainstream, fusion, experimental, New Age, harmolodic, jazz-funk, and ad infinitum items of stylistic dispute. Each jazz movement has its own highly opinionated coterie of fans, many of whom are unwilling to sit through examples of other styles, so jazz stations find it difficult pleasing the entire audience spectrum.

Jazz is found fulltime (or close to it) on many public radio stations, but its growth potential seems to lie in hybrid formats that combine it with AC, AOR, urban, or New Age. It also can work as a bloc format. A prominent CHR station, WQXI-FM in Atlanta, airs jazz on weekday evenings and scores enviable ratings. Adult contemporary radio station KIFM in San Diego also has registered healthy numbers with a similar scheme.

**MUSIC OF YOUR LIFE** is a syndicated pre-rock format that plays mostly big bands. It scored many impressive ratings triumphs half a decade ago, but has experienced more fleeting successes since.

**NEW AGE** (also known as NAC, for New AC or New Age Contemporary) is in its infancy, with a bandwagon of born-again New Age conversions following well-publicized experiments in Los Angeles, Washington, San Francisco, Chicago, and a few other locales. New Age music, mostly instrumental atmospheric records largely popularized by the Windham Hill label and characterized by unbelievers as "aural wallpaper" and "beautiful music for yuppies," has been a quiet industry phenomenon. It frequently sells well without significant radio or TV exposure. However, the jury is out on how it will work on the radio. Most stations are mixing it with jazz or AC or soft AOR programming. Nonmusical elements are generally minimal, with KTWV ("The Wave") in Los Angeles operating without air personalities. Early ratings results were mixed. It's safe to assume, however, that many of the bandwagon-jumpers who see NAC as an instant solution to years of ratings problems will fail, as happened with hasty converts to disco, classic rock, post–urban cowboy country, and countless other radio fads.

**NEWS** stations began about twenty-five years ago in New York, and have found a successful AM-only niche. Listeners in large markets have found it convenient to be able to tune in any time for a quick news update (all-news stations generally complete a news cycle in under a half hour). It's a lot cheaper to play records than maintain a big news staff, so news operations aren't generally feasible outside the big markets.

**NEWS/TALK** is simply a combination of news and talk programming: there are blocks filled by talk show hosts, and other times of the day ("dayparts," in radio argot) are taken up by extended newscasts. N/T is also an AM format, expensive to operate, but often successful in large markets.

**NOSTALGIA** essentially refers to stations playing pre-rock music exclusive of big band; for instance, the popular song stylists of the fifties. It is located under the easy listening umbrella in large-scale format analyses.

**QUIET STORM** represents a coming of age for black radio. In its forty-year existence, from "race" music to urban contemporary, black radio has been a cradle-to-grave format. The audience has never been large enough or sufficiently desirable economically to necessitate subformats by music style or demographic appeal. Now, although the spread is still limited, there are several stations programming a quiet storm approach. The name comes from the original "Quiet Storm" program on WHUR in Washington, on which Melvin Lindsay began playing a mixture of softer R&B, mostly ballads, and the mellower brands of jazz in the mid-seventies. Quiet Storm formats are aimed at adults (primarily black, but some stations attract considerable white listeners) who tire of the relentless upbeat pace of most urban stations. Many of these same urbans are now running quiet storm-type segments at night in order to attract this same audience.

**RELIGIOUS** as a format designation refers to religious talk programming, often the "dollar-a-holler" preacher-show airtime purchased by exposure-seeking evangelists directly from the stations. It's an inexpensive way to run a radio operation, and there's no shortage of people who want to hear the Word (nor of preachers who want to spread it), so religion remains a deeply entrenched radio format. The prudent tendency of wealthy religious organizations to buy radio stations of their own also contributes to the format's ubiquity.

**SPORTS** radio is about to receive its first exclusive station. At this writing, WFAN (formerly WHN) in New York—an AM outlet—is set to begin broadcasting a combination of play-by-play sports events (Mets baseball being the linchpin) and sports talk shows.

Many talk stations carry sports call-in shows, while play-by-play (PBP) sports, a staple of radio, air mostly on full-service ACs and news/talk outlets. Occasionally you'll hear live sporting events on CHRs, country stations, gold formats, and conceivably on every format in existence. Baseball is the leading PBP sports attraction, but all major sports can be heard, as well, no doubt, as lacrosse, curling, and the three-legged race at the local Elks picnic. A *Radio & Records* story on sports programming uncovered one station that claimed to air play-by-play fishing broadcasts, a pastime that would seem to rival championship chess for sheer radio drama.

**TALK** stations consist mostly of interactive call-in shows, with instructional programs often included as ballast. As with all nonmusic programming, talk shows are expensive to produce, and are thus limited mostly to major markets. Talk format audiences skew heavily toward the older end of the radio audience, but the most successful talk stations, often bolstered by sports, draw huge ratings (KABC in Los Angeles is a prominent example). They frequently generate disproportionate attention thanks to controversial, politically extreme hosts, and are true mainstays of the AM band (only one major talk station exists on FM, WWDB in Philadelphia).

Talk programs are commonly found on full-service AC stations, and the morning zoo entertainment-over-music trend in CHR and AOR wake-up shows has turned many nominal contemporary music shifts into virtual talk segments (shock jock Howard Stern, for example, rarely if ever plays a record on his WXRK/New York show, concentrating on phone bits and frequently off-color comedy interchanges with fellow cast members).

**URBAN CONTEMPORARY** started as a less negative name for the disco or dance music format, and evolved into a bridge between black radio and CHR. Now, thanks to negative selling by sales reps from rival formats, it has become a synonym for black radio. Most stations emphasizing black artists prefer the urban label, since many pioneering urbans were able to attract sizable numbers of white listeners and a bit more attention from ad agencies.

With more and more white artists working in traditionally black musical domains and earning airplay on those stations, urban is also probably a more accurate term than the limiting black radio. Some stations that cater exclusively to their local black communities (something many urbans pay little attention to as far as public service and supportive community relations go) wish to retain the black designation, but designs on white and Hispanic listeners as well as blacks influence most stations to use the urban euphemism.

Having absorbed the strains of dance music, funk, rap,

ballads, and everything in between, urban stations have made great strides in ratings; they are in the lead in several major markets. Economic prosperity has not kept pace, however, as ad agencies persist in viewing urban listeners as denizens of the underclass. Instead, the bulk of their advertising is placed with the more upscale CHRs, ACs, and even AORs. (Country suffers from a "white trash" form of this discrimination, though it's not as severe.)

Although Black Quiet Storm and Gold formats exist, the urban format is still not subject to much internal splintering. There's room for a bit of the blues at some Southern stations, which tend to be more receptive to rawer productions and smaller-label releases, and a few stations specialize in rap and hip-hop music, but most stations in the format play pretty much the full spectrum. On-air presentations generally resemble the CHR approach.

## WHY FORMATS, ANYWAY?

**A**fter plowing through descriptions of five dozen formats and subformats and subtle gradations and degradations, you might be excused for wondering why are there formats at all? It's all music, isn't it? Why don't radio stations just pick the best music from the entire field? That's how they do it in England and Europe. What purpose does all this specialization serve?

In music radio, formats exist in large part because the record industry finds them convenient. Radio and records coexist in an uneasy symbiosis, with each partner chasing different goals. Labels want to sell records. Radio stations want to sell commercial time. Ideally, labels get free exposure for their records on radio stations, who score good ratings by playing the hits and are thus able to sell more advertising. It's a neat synchromesh, and usually, but not always, it works.

# EXPLAINING THE
# INTERRELATIONSHIP

Labels like format radio. An urban station may not be able to play a record company's current country priority release, but there are plenty of country stations to do that. And airplay of an urban record on a station whose audience is largely urban record buyers sells a lot of product.

Extending that reasoning even further, labels like stations with tight (small) playlists. They will complain long and loudly about that so-and-so at K-blank who won't add any of their records, even if every other station in the region is banging them in power rotation. But they know that when that so-and-so at K-blank *does* add one of their records, his tight playlist ensures much more airplay exposure for the song. If he's in a major market, the additional exposure will translate into additional sales.

In a small market, however, the label will become genuinely annoyed at a station's restrictive policies. The extra rotations on the record played won't have any real sales effect, since there are few consumers to buy them. Labels would rather have small stations report airplay on a large number of records. Impressive totals of reported plays in trade publications, presenting a comparative national airplay picture, will influence other, larger stations to add the records to their playlists.

# EXPLORING
# CHARTED TERRITORY

Another reason labels like stations grouped according to formats is so the trade publications can create format charts by combining the airplay data from similarly-format-ted stations. Record companies like a *lot* of charts. The more charts there are, the more chances the label has to create a success story for a record. Since no record company reveals specific sales figures for a record, trade charts are the indus-try's report cards; if there's a chance for a second—or twelfth —opinion, they'll take it.

That's why there are charts for CHR, country, AC, urban, jazz, AOR (tracks and albums), and more, and dozens of pub-lications that create them, some armed with little more than a mimeograph and a high opinion of their ability to pick hits, but all supported to some extent by a generous (or opportu-nistic) record industry.

It may seem odd, but in the United States there is *no* chart providing an overall ranking of national airplay for current songs. (The *Billboard* Hot 100, which has pretensions of being such a chart, actually gathers most of its raw chart data from the same CHR stations used by other publications for their format-specific CHR charts.)

If there were a true national chart, combining all formats' hits, it would be nothing but a toy for the amusement of the public. The record industry couldn't use it. Mixing up CHR and country and urban and AC hits would produce a fruit salad chart—apples and oranges and everything in between.

Radio stations also find the format charts handy as guides to the records that work at other stations in the same format. The radio/record symbiosis works smoothly in this regard. Trade publications collate the airplay activity of each individ-ual record, converting the figures into chart positions. Some also list the total number of stations playing the song, those adding it that week, and the individual stations playing the record.

In combination with the station's own local research on the song's performance (requests, sales, results of callout re-search, etc.), this national perspective gives stations an ex-tremely detailed view of future hits and nonhits. It is a system driven by consensus, and though producing the weaknesses and abuses that stem from any consensus (herd mentality, reluctance to experiment, attempted manipulation), it's still, as I have opined previously, as close to the will of the people in action as you'll find in any communications medium.[3]

It is also a system, it should be pointed out, that makes substantial manipulation difficult and payola in the classic sense all but impossible. In an age of research and audience testing, the "my sister-in-law made this record and we're gonna make it a hit if we have to pay off every radio station in the country" scenario is dead in the water. Today's programmer will test a random sample of listeners' reaction to the sister-in-law's record, compare notes with other programmers who will also be testing the record and getting back negatives, and will decide playing the record is not worth the risk of alienating a substantial segment of his audience and jeopardizing the ratings upon which his job stands or falls.

The most a hypothetical payola campaign can accomplish for a bad record is influence over programmers to "paper-add" it to the playlists they supply to national trade publications. This might persuade other programmers to give the record a shot—briefly, until the results of their own tests come in and they note that the record isn't really moving anywhere else. At no time during this process does the record receive any significant actual airplay. Radio stations play records that work for them—that the audience is known to like, or that it is safe to assume the audience will come to like—based on an artist's past performance, test results, or evidence, gleaned through national trades, that the song is performing well elsewhere. Commentators looking to payola for an easy answer to their nagging convictions that most everything on the radio is crap would do better to assess the gap between their own advanced tastes and those of the listening audience.

# PRACTICAL PURPOSES
# OF FORMATTING

**A**side from the concerns of record companies, formatting is convenient for the radio industry as well. It's generally masked from the audience. Listeners don't tell their friends, "I listen to WNEW-FM becuse it's my favorite AOR station," or "B96 sure plays great CHR music," or "KLRS's innovative AC–New Age–jazz hybrid format never fails to relax me when I get home from work, while my daughter and her kitten enjoy that soft-rock ambience all day long." Stations don't generally promote their format designations on-air (country stations are a frequent exception); they'd rather be perceived as the station that plays your favorite songs.

But format designations provide a handle for the industry, especially the ad agencies. By classifying a station within one of the accepted formats, demographic and psychographic facts and figures associated with that format's listeners can be cited to bolster the station's sales story. In addition, even if a station doesn't assign a format designation to itself, perhaps feeling its programming is something unique that crosses traditional lines, the industry, for purposes of classification and analysis, will make its own designation.

(There's also a frivolous motivation for format identification. As in most industries, people enjoy creating impenetrable jargon only they, through constant use, can bandy. There is a certain sly pleasure in being able to tell a fellow industryite, "We're an innovative AC–New Age–jazz hybrid targeting 25-to-49-year-old women, children, and small household pets.")

# SIMPLE MATHEMATICS

The main reason for formatting is simply that ten thousand commercial radio stations compete for a relatively small portion (about 7 percent) of America's $110 billion media advertising budget.[4] Radio is far more competitive than TV, even with cable in the latter's picture, because there are eight times as many radio stations and, as just pointed out, a lot less money to go around. Individual stations face too much competition to be everything to everyone. Each has to carve out a piece of the market and position itself as a consistent, dependable source of something: news, information, new music, Punxsutawney's Best Rock, Carlsbad's Country Classics, Los Angeles's Smokin' Oldies. Listeners want reliability and reassurance from radio stations. They expect to hear their favorite song, or a bunch of others that sound a lot like it. The number of listeners who would be dazzled by inspired eclecticism is vastly exceeded by those who want to hear the top ten pop, country, urban, or rock hits.

Really, it all boils down to economics. Commercial radio stations are investments made by owners with two goals: selling enough advertising during the broadcast day to generate handsome profits for a steady, rising income, or making the station a desirably salable proposition.

Radio station owners come in three broad classes: small businessmen who own or share in one usually small-market outlet; large media companies owning chains of stations in small, medium, and/or major markets; and investors attracted to radio's potentially high profitability or quick, lucrative buy-build up-sell turnover. (While the vast majority of stations are marginally successful at best, when one hits big, the returns can be astronomical.)

Investors have become increasingly prominent in the industry in recent years. One reason for their prominence is the relaxation of U.S. regulations governing the number of stations that can be owned simultaneously (upped from fourteen to twenty-four, twelve AM stations, twelve FM), and how quickly a station can be sold after its purchase. (A three-year minimum between buying and reselling was eliminated, although the government may reimpose it.) In addition, the investment community's somewhat belated recognition of radio as an attractive speculative prospect has brought hundreds of new players into the field. Today, one in ten stations is traded within a year.

But whether the economic motive is long-term stability or fast turnover profit, the effect on programming is the same. The program director's mission is to find a format that delivers a healthy chunk of the demographically desirable (meaning, most likely, the 25-to-49-year-old age group) audience. With cutthroat competitors at every turn of the dial, all spending nearly equal amounts of time and money researching every aspect of modern radio—from positioning slogans, to music, to how many phone entries to take for call-in contests ("We'll take caller number 223 for a free Antarctic vacation") —the best that can be hoped for is a niche that can be protected and nurtured.

This dynamic breeds an odd sort of conservatism. Radio programming is largely conservative because years of meticulous research reveals that people like familiar music. In fact, research tells radio today that most people like familiar *older* music better than familiar-sounding new music.

Nineteen-eighty-six produced a surge of new oldies (gold) stations, particularly classic rockers specializing in late sixties and seventies AOR hits. But even the current-music formats, the ones that expose *some* new music, are finding that oldies provide a reassuring environment for listeners. And if increased gold rotations irk record labels—and they do: labels have practically washed their hands of AC as a record-selling format because of its high gold content; they engage in constant wars with country stations over their gold ratios; and have soured on AOR, just ten years ago the kingpin record-selling format, because of sharply reduced airtime for current records—well, too bad. Only urban and CHR remain current-music driven (with CHR wavering a bit), and those formats command only 27 percent of the total radio audience.[5] That starcrossed symbiosis between record labels, which get free advertising for their releases on radio, and radio, which gets free programming from labels, is unraveling.

# THE PIT AND
# THE PENDULUM

The huge number of American radio stations, along with the intricate peer-pressure construct of trade reporting that links them in tentative, cautious unity, has a potent, slow drag effect on pop music trends. The task of convincing hundreds of diverse and widespread stations to play the latest cultural phenomenon—at approximately the same time, so the record will accumulate enough airplay points to scale the charts—regularly traumatizes record labels. And it frustrates the dis-tant-early-warning specialists of the media who hop excitedly on the latest bandwagon just in time to watch it inch painfully through the great American radio swamp.

Sometimes, for example the British punk explosion of 1976–77, the revolutionary movement sinks almost trace-lessly, till a segment, its heartbeat faintly perceptible thanks to diehard journalists, is dredged from the depths by bowd-lerizers and forces of fashion to emerge as power pop or some other barely recognizable mutation. The original endures a subterranean existence, evolving into hardcore and speed metal, and surfacing from the pit now and again with only fleeting impact.

It takes time for a lightning-bolt music trend to saturate the nation, though an increasingly pop-mad media and national video channels make it easier (sometimes, as with the current heavy metal boom, without much help from radio). But American radio can still take a touted trend like Washington's go-go funk scene and bury it by sheer weight of inattention.

However, the present diversity of contemporary hit stations has created a new regionalism, a pendulum swing back to the days when new styles would sustain themselves in sympathetic territories until they broke out nationally. The best example today is the dance-oriented CHR networks in Miami, New York, and Los Angeles. Miami's Latino disco industry thrives, thanks to an active club scene and a powerful radio station, WPOW, which regularly makes citywide hits of the biggest club sensations. The cream of these hits is then picked off by radio sympathizers in New York and Los Angeles and later, sometimes, by the entire country. Acts like Exposé and Company B score national hits, while numerous other acts have multiple local smashes to tide them over while they wait for their break.

New York's own dance scene (though not its rap industry) also cross-fertilizes Miami and Los Angeles, while some West Coast hits surface through KPWR and spread to the other two dance bastions. National hits from this pipeline may be occasional, but the scene flourishes.

The new regionalism takes a different form in CHR-AOR, "modern rock" hybrids like KROQ in Los Angeles, KITS in San Francisco, and 91X in San Diego. These West Coast stations focus primarily on British acts, turning the Cure, Depeche Mode, and New Order into massive stars who can muster up only cult followings elsewhere. Sometimes a Pet Shop Boys will make the national superstar transition from the modern rockers. The path for others, as early 1988 midchart placings for the Cure and New Order demonstrated, is still treacherous, but again, the regional support base is in place for future assaults on the Top 10.

The problem is that the support base doesn't exist in very many places. The jury is still out about whether modern rock stations can succeed outside of the West Coast's progressive, well conditioned suburban sprawls. Dance CHRs seem tightly bound to cities with sizable tri-ethnic coalitions (of Hispanics, blacks, and whites) in which a station can get away with playing 80 percent dance material. But elsewhere, programmers are reluctant to tamper with CHR's delicate balance of pop, rock, ballads, and urban-dance music. All of which means the occasional standout innovation can break through, but trends will take time to establish, and 95 percent of the hits will continue to be music business as usual.

# DESPERATION BREEDS INNOVATION

Yet the same ferocious competition that forces conservatism on most stations inspires a certain relative radicalism in others. Every station would like to play a safe variety of familiar-sounding music to the broadest possible audience, but everyone can't. Too many stations are trying to hit the same bullseye.

Even successful stations are forced to fine-tune their formats constantly to adjust to new and established competition. But stations on the periphery are forced to experiment. Rather than expire as the fifth of five ACs in a market, they must attempt new approaches. That's why you can read about a half dozen or more format switches every week.

Most of the switching is effected within the same conservative boundaries; research will dictate, for example, that there's a hole for a classic rock station in the market. But slumping stations' desperation to find a new niche can breed innovation. In Los Angeles, for example, the influential dance-CHR hybrid format of KPWR arose in a facility that failed at various versions of AC and AOR for years, while the New Age trailblazer KTWV was a longtime "heritage" AOR—KMET—that had fallen on hard times.

When one of these longshots comes through, of course, the bandwagon effect comes into play, with any number of marginal stations deciding this hot new format will be the quick fix that will shoot their ratings to the stratosphere. Being marginal, these stations will usually try to cut corners, resulting in quick failures that undermine the national impact of the new format. But the point is that under a calm and conservative surface, there's a constant seething of refinement and radicalization in radio that does impel change.

Radio comes under attack from what we could call left- and right-wing bastions. On the left are the rock critic types who've never forgiven radio for growing out of the free-form, eclectic era, and resent the tight playlists and formatting of modern times. The right wing is made up predominantly of daily newspaper media critics who tend not only to disdain commercial radio but popular music itself. I recently found myself on a panel at an industry convention with several radio columnists from the dailies, and was dismayed to find that none of them *listened* to commercial radio beyond the occasional scan of a newscast; it was all cultured public radio on their dials. No wonder they raise highbrows at the Top 40.

Where the left and right wings meet is their conviction that the radio listener is being denied a *choice*, whether it be the chance to hear the latest Butthole Surfers opus on the top-rated CHR or AOR, or the opportunity to hear classical, jazz, or pre-rock pop crooners.

That choice is actually there, at least in bigger markets, where formats exist that play all those types of music (try your college station for the Surfers). But it is not commercial radio's mission to ennoble and uplift its listeners by offering an infinitely varied palette of varied musics (not that anyone could agree on just what is ennobling and uplifting, and what is irredeemable cultural garbage).

Commercial radio's mandate, dictated, it is true, by financial considerations, is to give its audience what it wants to hear. If the audience demands a profusion of oldies, so be it: the pendulum will swing the other way as soon as too many stations saturate the oldies-loving segment of the audience. Commercial radio is classic laissez-faire in action, and if that makes for lousy fare for the easily jaded opinion-makers who are privileged to air their feelings in print, it's of small consequence compared to a vast audience that is pleased with the comforts radio provides it.

The survival and continued success of the radio medium, despite a precarious economic situation and an unceasing barrage of competition from TV and other media, is a testament to a job well done. Most major markets can support one or perhaps two daily newspapers where, before television, four to six often existed, but there are many more commercial radio stations today than there were in the fifties.

Radio is best at creating illusions, and making them come true. Good air personalities convey the feeling that they're talking directly to you, without the distance inherent in other media. Your favorite station creates a comfortable environment for you, assuring you that it shares your concerns and will supply you with whatever you need to get through the day: a cheering human interest story, a tossed-off one-liner you can repeat at work, or outrageous blue material that makes you splutter in scandalized delight, "How can they *say* that on the radio?"

And your station convinces you, through constant repetition of slogans, that it's got more of *your* favorite music—six in a row coming up! So you sit through a stop set of three thirty-second commercials and a traffic report because you *know* you're going to hear your favorite song somewhere in that six-in-a-row sweep. And if your station has done its job—researched its listeners through constant contact with them to stay on top of their tastes—you *will* hear that favorite song. And an oldie you haven't heard for a while that sounds delightfully fresh. And a new song that sounds intriguing enough that you want to hear it again. That mix of music somehow sounds better than it could in any other medium you know. That incomparable feeling is the art—and science —of commercial radio.

# AIN'T NO

# MOUNTAIN HIGH ENOUGH

## *The politics of*

## *crossover*

**M**aybe it started with *Thriller*. It was certainly foreshadowed—if not catalyzed —by Prince's *Dirty Mind*, a lascivious black rock extravaganza from an artist whose band mixed up race and gender in unmistakably provocative ways. But wherever you locate the genesis of "crossover," by the late 1980s the American pop charts featured a more balanced combination of black and white music than at any time since the soul explosion of the late 1960s. In the 1986 *Billboard* year-end charts, black artists topped nine out of thirteen pop categories, as well as all the dance music categories; the year-end summary essay opened with the matter-of-fact observation that "Black music has been setting the pace in pop for the past four years." In mid-1987, the magazine inaugurated a Hot Crossover 30 chart, which codified changes in the composition of pop radio that had been taking shape since 1982. Perhaps most surprising of all, MTV officially opened its playlist to "dance" hits late in 1987.

In many ways these changes represented a gratifying reversal of recent history. During the interlude between the height of the (tacitly racist) antidisco backlash in 1978 and Michael Jackson's breakthrough in 1983, the charts had been as deeply segregated as at any time in the rock era. Not everyone greeted the reintegration with open arms, though. Crossover music soon came under attack on two main counts. Many critics charged a sellout of the tougher strains of black musical tradition—or of blackness itself: satirist Pedro Bell's cover art for George Clinton's *R&B Skeletons in the Closet* (1986) depicted such personal hygiene crossover aids as Barber Inna Bottle ("new nap-rid formula"), Tall Brite ("super strength skin lightener lotion"), and Holly Would Premium Cheese ("contains four washable smiles of durable plastic"). As if the point weren't clear enough, Bell also offers *Your Roots-Erasing Manual*: "Learn the secrets of putting your best face forward, even if it isn't yours!"

The rhetoric of the sellout isn't new; the crossover critic who decries synthesized pop-funk often echoes the 1960s folkies who bemoaned the rise of the electric guitar. The criticism is based on very narrow ideas about counts as authentic musical expression and what doesn't (soulful grunts are authentically black, pop crooning isn't); like the folkies before them, right-thinking opponents of crossover dutifully ignore changes in social relations, technology, and prevailing musical styles.

The second anticrossover position is rooted in the politics of black nationalism and black capitalism. Simply put, the erosion of racial barriers in the production, distribution, and consumption of black music poses an economic threat to the class of entrepreneurs and professionals who make their living from black music markets. This is a more complicated issue, and its place in the crossover debate is obscured by the fact that nationalist economic agendas are frequently submerged in arguments about musical authenticity.

Whatever the impetus, outcries against black and white musical miscegenation are nothing new. Ever since rock 'n' roll—the most popular expression of that miscegenation—became a national presence in 1954–55, it has been the subject of periodic attacks. For obvious reasons, the white voices ring louder through history. "We've set up a twenty-man committee to do away with this vulgar, animalistic, nigger rock 'n' roll bop," proclaims a man standing in front of a "We Serve White Customers Only" sign in the film *This Is Elvis*. "Our committee will check with the restaurant owners, and the cafes, to see what Presley records is on their machines, and then ask them to do away with them." Lest such voices from the 1950s seem like just so much antiquated barbarism, remember that it was just over ten years ago that Chicago disc jockey Steve Dahl started a near-riot at Comiskey Park with his "Disco Sucks" promotion, which was in essence a pep rally for bigots.

And lest it seem that the pre-1980s dissenting voices always belonged to white bigots, remember the 1968 National Association of Television and Radio Announcers (NATRA) convention. NATRA, an organization primarily composed of black radio and record industry personnel, had for years been a social gathering point for R&B business people, both black and white. But in 1968 the scene turned explosive. A more militant outcry for black professional and economic advancement was raised, and many whites at the convention found themselves threatened with physical violence. Atlantic Records exec (and R&B production pioneer) Jerry Wexler was hanged in effigy. Phil Walden, a young white businessman and soul afficionado who managed Otis Redding, later traced his decision to get out of black music and into white rock to his 1968 experience at NATRA. The NATRA debacle will figure in this story again, but for now let it stand as a symbol of the ambivalence toward crossover shared by many blacks—a subject nearly as complex and variegated as the history of the music itself.

The most persistent theme in anticrossover criticism eighties style is the neo-folkie notion that crossing over to pop success is inherently dangerous to a black artist's integrity, as well as to the "authenticity" of his or her music. It's a charge that's hardly ever explained; most often it arises in oblique, unfavorable comparisons between contemporary black performers and their antecedents. Journalist Andy Van de Voorde, whose essay "Crossing Over: Are Black Superstars Killing Black Music?"[1] is a useful summary of anticrossover arguments, captures the tone of this criticism when he sniffs: "Soul singer Percy Sledge certainly didn't sacrifice any of *his* blackness when he sang 'When a Man Loves a Woman' in 1966—but the record surprised everyone by going to Number One on the pop charts."

Pedro Bell's Clinton cover sounds a similarly contemptuous refrain in a list titled "Captain Crossover: What to Drop to Go Pop." According to this line, black artists who cross over must take certain elements *out* of their music and their self-presentation in order to make it palatable to white audiences. Just what they're taking out remains vague, but Bell implies that they become modern-day Stepin Fetchits to get across: among his Captain Crossover tips is the advice, "Do smile and appear grateful a lot when you get on teevee. It's besides-the-point that airbody's getting rich offa you and there's still no money to buy your mama a house, like you promised. . . ."

In many ways this line of attack is a verson of standard black nationalist rhetoric. As the basis for a musical aesthetic, it's absurd, since the criticism presumes a pure—and thus necessarily static—body of black music, and requires a set of culture czars qualified to distinguish "real" black music from "fake" black music. The internal contradictions in this outlook are nowhere more evident than in the case of black rocker Vernon Reid. Reid first gained attention by forming the Black Rock Coalition, an organization dedicated to shattering industry and audience preconceptions about black music; he added an exclamation point to the BRC platform in early 1988 when his band, Living Colour, released a striking hard rock album. Yet Reid is also one of the most vocal critics of a perceived sellout of blackness in many crossover hits. This puts him in a dubious position: on the one hand, railing against narrow conceptual biases about what black music can be; on the other, claiming that a large portion of contemporary black pop is not *legitimately* black. It's easy to condemn the schlock produced in recent years by Lionel Richie, to be sure. But it's impossibly patronizing to suggest that his music isn't a "genuine" variety of black pop. It's a conceptual dead end, too, leaving little room to affirm evolution and change in any direction.

And whatever else you care to say about black pop, it has certainly undergone changes in the 1980s, influenced by factors as varied as hip-hop styles and rhythms, white rock, the advent of new digital music-making technologies, and changes in popular radio formats that give blacks greater access. These developments are bound to be offensive and disorienting to purists. Enter Peter Guralnick, a critic-historian who is unsurpassed in his appreciation of older American forms (blues, country, fifties R&B, sixties soul). In the paraphrase of Van de Voorde, Guralnick claims that nowadays "many young [black] performers are too hip for their own good, and their painfully self-conscious attempts to emulate whatever movement they feel is hot at the moment stunt their own musical growth."[2]

It's certainly true that any young artist signed to a record deal is subjected to pressures that may distort his or her musical vision, but the phrase that leaps out of Guralnick's formulation is the allusion to artistic self-consciousness as limiting and even painful for black performers. By way of contrast, he refers to the 1960s Stax Records experience as an instance in which the artists didn't have "any idea what they were doing, what they were groping for." (To suggest this of Otis Redding—to pick only one example—seems incomprehensible on its face, but that's another matter.) As Guralnick must know, this sort of Portrait of the Artist as a Young Natural comes perilously close to the noble-savage stereotype used historically to undermine the achievements of blacks. (Detroit Pistons basketball star Isiah Thomas drew public attention to this kind of bigotry after the 1987 NBA playoffs, when he complained bitterly of the media's differential treatment of white players—"smart" athletes—and black players—"natural" athletes.)

Such an outlook simply can't comprehend what's going on in black pop today. Despite the outcries of its critics (many of whom maintain paradoxically that it all sounds alike, *and* that it's too prone to splintering along the lines of the latest trends), black pop in the late 1980s is remarkable for its stylistic eclecticism. There is the funky black rock of Prince, Cameo, and Alexander O'Neal; the balladry of Freddie Jackson and Anita Baker; the girl-group romanticism of Lisa Lisa and Cult Jam; and a veritable explosion of dance tracks and remixes, expertly crafted by more than a dozen different producers.

Just as white rock has grown more reflexively conscious of its own history in the past fifteen years (Bruce Springsteen, who is forever lifting titles and images from old songs, is the clearest example), so has black pop. On its surface, the idea of reflexivity connotes a kind of circuitous formalism—new songs *about* old songs—but in practice this reflexivity has produced intriguing and often revelatory results. To return to Springsteen for a moment, his "Racing in the Street" comments not only upon a song by Martha and the Vandellas and a mythic vision by Brian Wilson; it also surveys the lives of the people who consumed those records and myths.

Likewise, rapper Kool Moe Dee's "No Respect," which appropriates Otis Redding/Aretha Franklin's "Respect," is on one level a subversive homage to an old record. At the same time, it's a commentary on how ill-realized the aspirations expressed in that old record still remain. The list goes on, and it's not restricted to rap. Full Force's delightful *Guess Who's*

*Coming to the Crib* (1987) surveys (and frequently lampoons) the recent black pop scene, from macho rap posturings to crossover politics to Morris Day and the Times pastiches. The point here is not to argue for the relative virtues of reflexive art, but to show that this kind of reflexivity can only happen as a matter of self-conscious design. Black music, now as ever, is very much self-conscious artistry.

Though almost all of the anticrossover criticism in the eighties is cast in terms of a debate about "authentic" black music versus "fake" black music, that doesn't mean the real issue is always aesthetic. One of the most vocal critics in recent years has been Nelson George, *Billboard*'s black music columnist and author of the Motown history *Where Did Our Love Go?* In his work, a black nationalist agenda is never far from the surface, though he rarely mentions it by name; rather, it's there to be inferred from the sum of his views.

George has described crossover as the product of "black American singers [who] want to be Barry Manilow," and the symbolism evoked by his analogy to the supreme purveyor of banal white pop is emphatic: not only does crossover amount to a kind of cultural treason, blacks who have consistent pop hits necessarily sacrifice their racial identity. What's the alternative, George? Well, he points favorably toward 1973, when such "intrinsically black songs" as Marvin Gaye's "Let's Get It On" and the Isley Brothers' "Who's That Lady" cracked the pop Top 10. "And that," he adds, "was before disco, and before record labels got interested in black music." He also mentions the example of Frankie Beverly and Maze, whose records have frequently gone gold without much attention from white audiences. And he says this about radio: "It's a fallacy that you need a big [pop] single to reach white people. Plenty of white people listen to black radio."[3]

If it seems curious to assert that "record companies" weren't interested in black music in 1973, if it seems misleading to claim you can reach the white pop audience to a significant degree through black radio—if it's hard to find any consistent aesthetic thread running through his commentary about music—that's because the real issue is more economic than musical. It's of more than passing interest to note that George's examples of authentic black music from 1973 were both released on black-owned record labels (Gordy's Motown, and the Isley's own T-Neck), and that what he finds inspirational about Maze is the group's ability to have gold records with an almost all-black audience. Conversely, one reason George disdains crossover is that the creeping integration of record charts and major label artist rosters threatens to undermine the interests of black entrepreneurs by gnawing simultaneously at their traditional markets and their productive resources.

It's a serious issue and—in American capitalism more generally—an old one. But it's highly disingenuous of George to conceal this agenda in a series of harangues about musical standards; it lets him circumvent the tough questions. His remark about black radio is symptomatic. When he points out that you can reach some white listeners through black radio, what he's really suggesting between the lines, of course, is that black radio is the proper home for black records. Yet as *The Discordant Sound of Music,* the NAACP's 1987 report on racism in the music industry, indicates, "Of the more than 9,000 radio stations in the country, fewer than 400 target their programming to black listeners, so that the market for black artists is limited to less than 30 million people in a country of over 230 million people."

The manifest appeal of George's argument to black capitalism is clear, but so is the extent to which his vision would harden the lines that keep black artists and black audiences in segregated economic ghettos. For every black artist who becomes a crossover success, he elaborates, "there are many more who fail. Everyone wants to be Michael Jackson. But very few people understand the nature of record companies —that there are very few people who reach 'that [level of success]."[4]

If George were commenting generally on the record industry's version of late capitalism, in which fewer and fewer products are released to more and more hype, he'd have a point. But he's speaking in specifically racial terms, and his implicit point—which can hardly be made explicit since it isn't true—is that black artists would stand a better chance of succeeding with small labels, or with record divisions that appeal to principally black markets. Small independent labels are very often undercapitalized, which makes them less able to pay and promote artists. It is no accident that artists tend to flee these smaller labels for larger ones as soon as the opportunity presents itself; the chances to make money and gain exposure are that much greater (even if, in absolute terms, they still aren't that great). As crossover possibilities opened up in the 1980s, a number of black independent labels—most notoriously, Sylvia Robinson's Sugar Hill Records —saw their artists migrate to major labels.

The 1987 NAACP report on racism in the music business was in part a response to these economic changes. It called attention to a number of long-standing imbalances: Blacks are underrepresented in the industry, it said, especially in professional and managerial positions; blacks receive less pay for comparable work; black concert promoters and radio stations are consistently bypassed in the promotion of major black artists; labels spend too little money with minority businesses and contractors and less money promoting black artists through means such as video than they spend on white artists; and black stars have too few black professionals on their payrolls.

But the report was almost as remarkable for the injustices it didn't mention. It said nothing of the exclusion of blacks from jobs ranging from secretary to engineer; nor did it take into account the cold statistical fact that, according to the Census Bureau, the average black American has only one-twelfth the economic assets of the average white, making equal participation in the consumption of popular music impossible.

Rather, the report concentrated almost exclusively on the problems of black professionals and entrepreneurs, whose interests have always been the main concern of the NAACP.

The NAACP's historical role as champion of the black middle class underlines a central problem of black capitalism (a problem exacerbated by the characteristically American failure to view racial issues in class terms): While black enterprise has offered a means of advancement for one (fairly small) group of blacks, it is predicated on the continued existence of segregated black markets. Yet the black working class has always preferred integration, seeing in it a better chance at decent schools, safe neighborhoods, and steady employment. Even at the height of black nationalist fervor in the late 1960s, leaders such as H. Rap Brown and Stokeley Carmichael had the support of only 15 percent of black Americans; more recently, a 1987 New York Times poll found that just 12 percent of U.S. blacks would prefer living in neighborhoods that were all or mostly black.

This schism has come to light time and again in recent decades. Martin Luther King founded the Southern Christian Leadership Conference (SCLC) largely because the NAACP opposed mobilizing blacks to fight for civil rights. And even when the NAACP did become involved in the struggle, its focus was different from the more radical groups. In one emblematic gesture, the Atlanta chapter in the early 1970s abandoned its demands for desegregation in exchange for a promise of more black administrative positions in the school system. The national body eventually suspended chapter head Lonnie King, Jr., and some of his cohorts for striking this bargain, but the Atlanta chapter was only practicing a more extreme version of what the organization had preached for a long time.

The violent separatism that dominated the 1968 NATRA convention I mentioned earlier was the product of an era when black music was more popular and profitable than ever before, and when then the legal progress achieved in civil rights during the 1960s was leading many people to believe that effective integration was possible and even, perhaps, not so far away. More than anything else, the NATRA reaction signified the black middle class's fear that their markets were irreparably eroding, and their recognition that most of the money produced by black pop was not ending up in *their* pockets. Phil Walden related to Peter Guralnick his memories of the racial lines drawn there:

I went to the convention. [White New Orleans entrepreneur] Marshall Sehorn got beaten up in the shower. I got threatened. The Fair Play Committee came up and said, "You making too much money." I kind of laughed. Then this black DJ told me, "That's one of the guys they pulled off the plane going to Chicago, because he was going to kill Elijah Muhammad. You better get away from him." One guy really hurt me, a black guy we had helped get two or three jobs as a DJ—he was finally in a major market—and he just hit me with this constant barrage of crap, this racist-slanted stuff, some insinuation that I was probably responsible for Otis's death—it made me *sick*. And it made it really hard for me to maintain a real interest, when I saw all the things I worked for being destroyed, Dr. King killed, and someone like me being hit with more racist stuff than George Wallace ever was. It made me SICK. You know, if I was a young black, I'd probably have been the most militant sonofabitch in the black race. But I just got tired of being called whitey and honky, because I knew in my heart what I had done, and I knew in my heart I was right.

The first time I heard the Rolling Stones, I said, "You've got to be kidding. Who'd want to be listening to this when you could be listening to a great soul singer?" But after that I just decided I'd get into white rock 'n' roll, and that's what I did.[5]

In the divisions it fostered, NATRA was not exactly unprecedented. Throughout this century, black separatism has provided an ideological warrant for black capitalism. From Marcus Garvey to Muslim spokesman Louis Farrakhan, the most militant champions of separatist black nationalism have been equally zealous proponents of black enterprise. *The Autobiography of Malcolm X* is full of passages that amplify the Muslim line on black capitalism: "Our businesses sought to demonstrate to the black people what black people could do for themselves—if they would only unify, trade with each other, exclusively where possible—and hire each other, and in so doing, keep black money within black communities."[6] Later: "As other ethnic groups have done, let the black people, wherever possible, however possible, patronize their own kind, hire their own kind, and start in these ways to build up the black race's ability to do for itself. . . . One thing the white man can never give the black man is self-respect!"[7] And, more succinctly: "It's because black men don't own and control their own community's retail establishments that they can't stabilize their own community."[8]

More recently, Jesse Jackson's Chicago-based PUSH (People United to Serve Humanity) has espoused a similar vision. PUSH and its predecessor, the Southern Christian Leadership Conference's Operation Breadbasket, were dedicated to advancing black business and professional interests through a two-pronged approach: by organizing massive black boycotts of major consumer goods producers, which lasted until the producer agreed to add more black employees to its staff, and by insisting that retail chains feature black-manufactured products prominently on their shelves.

During his lifetime, Martin Luther King helped to moderate Operation Breadbasket's latent economic separatism, but once he was gone, Jackson moved steadily in that direction. Under Jackson's leadership Breadbasket (and later PUSH) promoted such holidays as Black Christmas and Black Easter, imbuing them with their own special symbolism (such as the substitution of "Black Soul Saint" for Santa Claus) and urging blacks to patronize only black businesses in their holiday shopping. Later he organized Black Expo, a trade fair for black businesses.

In view of the four centuries of black experience in America, the appeal of nationalist rhetoric about pride, unity, and economic self-help is clear. But the real economics of separatism are more troublesome. The central premise, after all, is that a separatist black economic community will serve the interests of all blacks in a way that capitalism generally does not. But it's impossible to abstract black capitalism from its place in the larger matrix of industrial capitalism. Historically, the black working class in the United States has functioned much like the labor pool of a colonized nation, providing a source of cheaper labor that helped to depress the wage scale for all workers.

To remedy this split and achieve genuinely radical reform would require class unity between black and white workers; so long as these workers remain separated along lines of race, it works to the advantage of black and white capitalists alike. And the black working class, being far more economically depressed from the outset, suffers proportionately more. As historian C. Vann Woodward has pointed out, "The myth of black unity obscured the special interest of the black bourgeoisie as beneficiaries of racial separatism. . . . Advocates of 'black community control' were not black workers, but aspiring Negroes with an eye on administrative posts in public office, schools, hospitals, and social services. Their success would gratify racial pride, but it left the community with the same problems of poverty, unemployment, bad housing, and inferior schools. . . . Left intact, the black ghetto served as a kind of tariff wall to protect a monopolized market."

From Garvey to Malcolm X, one premise of nearly every nationalistic program is that black entrepreneurs would use their assets to build a community infrastructure that would embrace all blacks, rich and poor alike. The trouble with such sentimental utopianism is that it runs counter to the internal logic of capitalism itself, which dictates that the entrepreneur be an accumulator of capital first, and a promoter of community interests second—if at all. That's why the tale of Berry Gordy and Motown Records, the most dramatic success story in the annals of black enterprise, poses difficulties for black nationalism.

When Gordy launched Motown in the late 1950s, it was of necessity a family affair. Gordy's siblings and friends formed the core of the nascent operation, which was based in an unremarkable-looking house on Detroit's West Grand Boulevard. As Motown began to reach undreamed-of successes in the 1960s, however, it became clear that what Gordy had in mind was not a great experiment in communal black enterprise, but something decidedly more colorblind—The Sound of Young America, as it was emblazoned on the Motown logo. Gordy's insistence on a popular music that would cross entrenched color lines is one of Motown's most glorious legacies, and no one could argue with his success. Further, as Dave Marsh has pointed out, Gordy's systematic approach to career development gave many Motown acts a longevity that none of their black contemporaries on other labels even approached.

But when more and more white executives began to appear around the Hitsville offices, many blacks reacted bitterly. And when Motown pulled up stakes to move to Los Angeles in the early 1970s, many of the same people charged a desertion of the Detroit black community that spawned Motown in the first place. Ironically, it is Nelson George who has most concisely defined what Gordy was reaching for from the beginning, and what his critics failed to understand: "He was preaching success in 1963, not black success."

No matter what the color of its advocates, the American legacy of segregation has done more than merely shape events in our history; it has also distorted the telling of our real history. Nowhere is this more apparent than in the story of early rock 'n' roll. The conventional explanation (perpetually invoked, rarely explored) is that rock 'n' roll burst on the scene in the mid-fifties as an organic response to the baby boom. In this formulation, the music was the voice of a self-conscious, rebellious generation of unprecedented size and affluence, rock 'n' roll as collective id. This explanation has an undeniable neatness, as well as a certain validity. But it ignores another development of equal or greater importance, America's changing racial equation. Just as the migration of rural southern blacks to northern urban defense plants during World War II led to the first faltering steps toward the integration of baseball, so did it point toward the integration of commercial music. The concentration of blacks in cities made them a commercial market in a sense they hadn't been before; the diffuse "race music" market of the South became a thriving urban R&B market.

In the decade after the war, more and more small labels sprung up to exploit the R&B boom. In New York there was Atlantic Records, founded by two Turkish immigrant brothers in 1947, which became *the* premier R&B label; but otherwise the city produced surprisingly few important R&B independents. Instead the indies were scattered throughout the country, with concentrations in the West and Midwest. Chicago was home to Chess Records and VeeJay; Detroit had Fortune; Houston boasted several small labels, including Don Robey's Duke/Peacock. Los Angeles was the uncontested boomtown, however, producing such important R&B labels as Modern, Specialty, Imperial, and Aladdin. Moreover, during this same period the FCC was granting an unprecedented number of new radio licenses, creating a demand for new programming and giving R&B proportionately more exposure.

As a result, whites were exposed to black music (and vice versa) on a greater scale than ever before. Some black artists —mostly conservative, Tin Pan Alley stylists—were already having hits with white audiences: the Mills Brothers, the Ink

Spots, Ella Fitzgerald, Nat King Cole, Lena Horne. It's true that when the rock 'n' roll boom struck in earnest in 1954–55, teenagers accounted for an overwhelming part of its market; the music couldn't have become the commercial force it did without them. But rock-as-youth-culture can't explain the particular shape the music took, or the forces that had been leading to it for years, because those forces were more racial than generational.

Most histories of rock have little to say about the racial dynamics of its origins, but the truism I alluded to earlier (that early rock 'n' roll amounted to black invention and white theft/cooptation) still persists. There's a lot of truth in this observation, and it's probably necessary to insert a caveat here: as I talk about the interaction of black and white music in America, which seems to me remarkably rich and extensive given the racist setting in which it occurred, I don't mean to imply that black and white musicians have received anything approaching equal rewards—either in money or acclaim—for their talents. They have not.

But to jump from that fact to the conclusion that the story of American music is the story of "original" black music and "derivative" white imitations is too far a leap. For one thing, it's telling that the proponents of this line are so frequently opponents in principle of popular culture itself. Albert Goldman's 1981 Elvis biography makes much of the (untrue) allegation that Elvis's early hits were note-for-note copies of black records or other people's demos, but his point is not to celebrate Wynonie Harris and Big Mama Thornton; it's to deflate Elvis. What of the black artists in question? It isn't hard to see what a mindset that refuses to admit of poor southern whites creating art will make of poor southern blacks. In this view they're usually construed (even by ostensible admirers) as unselfconscious primitives acting out their natural rhythm and musicality.

Besides its overtones of racism and class hatred, this portrait of rock 'n' roll does enormous violence to American musical history. It reduces a complex dialectical relationship in which blacks and whites have mutually influenced each other to a simple instrumental one. Far more representative of the real picture is the story of Leiber and Stoller's "Hound Dog," cited by both Greil Marcus and Charles Hamm (whose indispensable *Music in the New World* brings together much of the historical information discussed here). Here is Marcus's version:

> **Jerry Leiber and Mike Stoller were Jewish boys from the East Coast who fell in love with black music. Hustling in Los Angeles in the early fifties, they wrote "Hound Dog," and promoted the song to Johnny Otis, a ruling R&B bandleader who was actually a dark-skinned white man from Berkeley who many thought was black. Otis gave the song to [Big Mama] Thornton, who recorded it in a slow bluesy style, and Otis also took the composer's credit, which Leiber and Stoller had to fight to get back. Elvis heard the record, changed the song completely, from the tempo to the words, and cut Thornton's version to shreds.**
>
> **Whites wrote it; a white made it a hit. And yet there is no denying that "Hound Dog" is a "black" song, unthinkable outside the impulses of black music, and probably a rewrite of an old piece of juke joint fury that dated back far beyond the birth of any of these people. Can you pull justice out of *that* maze?**[9]

Perhaps the most surprising thing about this story is that it's not anomalous, just concise. There were many others like it. That's worth remembering; at a remove of thirty years-plus, it's easy to lose track of the remarkable biracial composition of the first wave of rock 'n' roll. From 1955–58, the roster of popular rock 'n' rollers was more racially equal than at any time before or since. Chuck Berry, Little Richard, the Coasters, The Platters, Fats Domino, Lloyd Price—major stars

all, and on a rough par with the likes of Bill Haley, Jerry Lee
Lewis, and Buddy Holly.

In those days, as Hamm points out, the industry conceived
of three distinct and exclusive pop music audiences. The white
middle-class urban audience went mostly for Tin Pan Alley
standards, the black audience consumed R&B, and rural
southern and midwestern audiences bought country records.
*Billboard* charts were structured accordingly. Rock 'n' roll tore
up these boundaries, producing records that hit on two or
even all three of the major charts. Elvis's "Hound Dog" went
Number One on both the country and R&B charts, and later
hits by the Everly Brothers, Jerry Lee Lewis, Johnny Horton,
and (of course) Elvis topped all three charts. No black rocker
pulled off the triple crown, because the country audience
steadfastly rejected black performers; strangely, though,
many blacks responded favorably to rockabilly, a combination of countrified instruments and heated R&B rhythms.

Musically, rock 'n' roll realized trends that had been shap-
ing up in R&B and country for years. The jump blues bands of
Lionel Hampton and Louis Jordan prefigured the early rock
groups in rhythmic energy and instrumental lineup, as did
hits like Wynonie Harris's "Good Rockin' Tonight," T-Bone
Walker's "Stormy Monday" (both 1947), and Jackie Brenston's
"Rocket 88" (a 1951 hit written and arranged by the young
Ike Turner). On the country side, the beat-heavy twang of such
early Bill Haley hits as "Crazy, Man, Crazy" (1953) and
"Happy Baby" (1954) suggested a similar direction. And if
you go back through old Hank Williams records, you'll find a
few sides that *are* rock 'n' roll, just as surely as if Williams
had lived to see the day—including "Move It on Over," "Mind
Your Own Business" (both 1949), and the amazing "Settin'
the Woods on Fire" (1952).

One demarcation point of rock 'n' roll wasn't really musical;
it came when black and white audiences started listening to
the music together. Alan Freed started playing black and
white music side by side on Cleveland's WWJ in 1951, and

by 1953 he began promoting package shows that featured racially-mixed bills with as many as seven or eight acts. At the first one, held in March of that year, a racially-mixed crowd of 75,000 turned out for a show in an auditorium that held less than one-third that many. Similarly mixed audiences usually turned out when he took the show on the road to other cities. Virtually all early rockers played to mixed audiences when they toured.

Those early Freed package shows were amazing for the unprecedented integration of the performers and fans as much as the music, and for the sense of discovery communicated on both levels. Someone recently gave me three volumes, long out of print, of *Alan Freed's Rock 'n' Roll Dance Party*. No dates are given, but the shows must be from 1956–57; the first volume includes Chuck Berry doing "Maybellene," the Johnny Burnette Trio tearing up "Oh Baby Babe" (which is really "Baby Let's Play House," but with this lyric amendment: "Come back, baby, I wanna make love to you"), and a stunning "Please Be Mine" by Frankie Lymon and the Teenagers. And on the back sleeve, surrounded by publicity photos of the mostly black groups on the bill, is a tight shot of two white teenage girls screaming ecstatically.

Hot stuff. Especially when you consider that these shows were happening less than a year after the Supreme Court ordered (in *Oliver Brown vs. Board of Education of Topeka*) the "good faith implementation" of school desegregation, and a full eight years before Alabama governor George Wallace proclaimed "segregation now, segregation tomorrow, segregation forever." Rock 'n' roll was the first place where American blacks and whites began to approach genuine, willful integration, and if that point has been lost or undervalued through the years, it certainly wasn't lost on *anyone* at the time. White supremacists correctly saw the music as an assault on their most deeply cherished values. "The obscenity and vulgarity of the rock 'n' roll music is obviously a means by which the white man and his children can be driven to the level with the nigger," said the Executive Secretary of the Alabama White Citizens Council in a 1950s newsreel clip. *"It is obviously negro music."*

Avowed bigots weren't alone in their discomfiture, either. In more encoded ways, the northern press reacted with fear and disdain to the racial ferment taking place. Alluding to the nonsense syllables commonly used by black vocal groups, a *Denver Post* editorial writer (quoted in the July 23, 1956, issue of *Time*) pronounced, "This hooby-dooby, oop-shoop, ootie ootie, boom boom de-addy boom, scoobledy gobbledy dump—is trash." The reaction had overtones of class as well as race. A relatively more erudite *Time* staffer made vicious fun of the music's roots in the styles of poor southerners, black and white: rock 'n' roll, he said, "underlines the primitive qualities of the blues with malice aforethought. Characteristics: an unrelenting, socking syncopation that sounds like a bullwhip; . . . a vocal group that shudders and exercises violently to the beat while roughly chanting either a near-nonsense phrase or a moronic lyric in hillbilly idiom."

Beyond eroding racial barriers, rock 'n' roll also disrupted the prevailing mode of production in the record industry. Tin Pan Alley music was a cumbersome beast, involving professional songwriters and lyricists, arrangers and copyists, and full orchestras with conductors. As Hamm points out, "All this was threatened by rock 'n' roll. Since it was an oral music, not written down, performed by a small number of players who had the music in their heads or improvised it on the spot, there was no need for arrangers, studio orchestras, or copyists. . . . It was a simple, efficient, effective system. And it threatened the jobs of many thousands of people." [10] The industry first disparaged rock 'n' roll (Columbia's Mitch Miller was the most vocal spokesman); then, as they saw the charts taken over by small-label rock 'n' roll hits, they adapted to it by releasing a spate of homogenized "rock 'n' roll" records of their own.

These records are infamous: Doris Day's "Tweedle Dee";

Georgia Gibbs's "Rock Right"; the Crew Cuts's "Sh-Boom"; and Pat Boone's string of abominable covers, including Fats Domino's "Ain't That A Shame," Little Richard's "Tutti Frutti," the El Dorados' "At My Front Door," *ad nauseam.* They're worth mentioning here only because they come up so frequently when the history of white profiteering from black creativity is being discussed. That's exactly what happened in many cases, particularly that of the dread Boone, but it's important to keep in mind the context. The most egregious rip-offs weren't a dominant part of rock 'n' roll's first wave, but part of a calculated reaction to it; for every execrable cover of an R&B tune, in other words, there was an original piece of schlock so musically anaesthetized it was impossible to tell whether it derived from black music or white. And second, to the extent that the Pat Boone syndrome was genuinely a racial reaction, it was a reaction to the unprecedented *integration* being lived out in this new music, and by its fans.

So far as symbols of early rock 'n' roll are concerned, few can rival the Sun Records label, with its orange, yellow, and black image of a rooster crowing and the sun rising. Designed by Jay Parker, a Memphis man who played in the same high school band with label founder Sam Phillips, it's an image that has come to *mean* early rock 'n' roll to many people. Phillips's own description of it pretty aptly summarizes the place of Sun Records in rock 'n' roll mythology: "The sun to me, as a kid on the farm . . . I'd hear the rooster crow and see the sunrise and it was a universal kind of thing. A new day, new opportunity, you know."

There's no denying the historical importance of Sun. Such seminal early rockers as Jerry Lee Lewis, Carl Perkins, and Johnny Cash got started in the studio at 706 Union Avenue in Memphis. And before they came along, Phillips spent a few years cutting blues and country sides (many of them distinguished, few of them renowned). But of course Elvis is the main reason we remember Sun Records, and we remember it for what he represented: a revolutionary fusion of black and white music whose time had come. And that's correct, so far as it goes. Yet Sun's appeal as a mythic symbol—in some ways, *the* mythic symbol—of the era is more than a matter of historical recognition. In contrast to the racially mixed reality of mid-1950s rock 'n' roll, Sun Records in its glory days was almost entirely white, and the accretions of myth have made it even more so. As such, it's a symbol equally well-suited to the exclusionists, who simply want to ignore blacks' role in the music, and to the instrumentalists, who want to claim that rock 'n' roll was a unilateral rip-off, a paler shade of R&B.

The Sun mythology *doesn't* capture the leading role of blacks in the evolution of the new popular music, or their ongoing role in its development. Nor does it suggest the mutualism with which these mostly southern, mostly working-class black and white musicians influenced each other. The enterprises that most sharply symbolized that side of the story came along five or ten years later; they were located across town, in Memphis' old Capitol Theater at 926 East McLemore, and further south, in Muscle Shoals, Alabama.

Stax Records in Memphis was started by a brother and sister team, Jim Stewart and Estelle Axton, in 1960. For some time the old Capitol Theater doubled as both makeshift recording facility and neighborhood record shop; Fame (an acronym for Florence Alabama Music Enterprises) Music in Muscle Shoals had an even less auspicious beginning. Its first studio was over a drugstore, in a former podiatrist's office that was still strewn with plaster casts of feet when Tom Stafford, Rick Hall, and Billy Sherrill moved in and started stapling egg cartons to the walls for acoustic effect. This was in 1959, and most of the principals were barely out of their teens.

The Stax (then Satellite) label had its first hit in late 1960, with the teenaged Carla Thomas's "Gee Whiz." Fame didn't incorporate as a label, but the first hits produced there came in 1962, and they were modest: Arthur Alexander's "You Better Move On," and Jimmy Hughes's "Steal Away." Both Stax and Fame were shoestring operations, like most of the independent music ventures of the day. By the mid-1960s, though, the Stax-Muscle Shoals axis was the southern counterpart to Motown, and all parties were succeeding beyond their wildest dreams—well, maybe not Berry Gordy's wildest dreams—as soul became a major force in American music. (Both Stax and Fame were integrally tied to Atlantic Records; Atlantic distributed Stax, and cut a number of sides at Fame, which had since moved out of the drugstore and grown so big that it eventually produced a spinoff, Quin Ivy's Muscle Shoals Studio.) It's hard to think of a non-Motown soul act whose path never led to either Memphis or Muscle Shoals. Otis Redding *was* Stax in the minds of many people; Aretha Franklin cut her epochal early Atlantic sides with Muscle Shoals personnel; Wilson Pickett recorded in Memphis *and* Muscle Shoals; and a whole stable of greater and lesser luminaries passed through, including Sam and Dave, Eddie Floyd, James Carr, Joe Tex, Arthur Conley, and Percy Sledge.

It's not surprising that the principal owners of all these operations were white. But here's the kicker: the nucleus of creative personnel at each place was integrated. Check any greatest hits collection by Otis, Aretha, Wilson Pickett, or Solomon Burke, and you'll find a number of the following men (all white) credited as writer, producer, player, or all three: Chips Moman, Dan Penn, Spooner Oldham, Steve Cropper, Duck Dunn, Tommy Cogbill, Jim Dickinson, Bobby Emmons, Jimmy Johnson. The Stax R&B instrumental group Booker T. and the MGs consisted of two black men, Booker T. Jones and Al Jackson, Jr., and two white men, Steve Cropper and Duck Dunn.

Superficially, it would be easy enough to pass off this integration as something imposed on black artists by white bosses, but that's simply not true. Nearly all the white players came from backgrounds that mixed up country and R&B in reckless fashion, and many had played in proto-R&B bands since high school. Besides, if you believe that these men were cut of a different cloth, that they weren't expressing the *same* heritage as their black colleagues on some level, then how can you account for such a wondrous piece of gospel-soul as Aretha Franklin's "Do Right Woman, Do Right Man," written by Dan Penn and Chips Moman? Or any of the songs cowritten by Otis Redding and Steve Cropper? Or Duck Dunn's bass playing? As Peter Guralnick wrote in summation of his research for *Sweet Soul Music*, a history of southern soul in the 1960s, "The picture I got . . . showed not so much the white man in the woodpile, or even the white businessman capitalizing on social placement and cultural advantage to plunder the resources of a captive people, as the white *partner* contributing as significantly as his more prominent—more visible certainly—black associate."[11]

If black and white musics in the South had never been so collaborative in a hands-on, day-to-day sense before, their histories were still inextricably linked. The miscegenation didn't commence with Stax, or Sun, or for that matter with the invention of the phonograph. Rather, it dated back to the early nineteenth century, and before. While the precise history of the various black and white folk musics is impossible to trace—this was oral, improvisational music, created and transmitted by people who were illiterate, enslaved, or both; there weren't even any music publishers of note in the South until the second half of the twentieth century—some of its outlines are apparent.

In the most general sense, we know that the first recorded blues, country, gospel, and jazz (circa 1920–40) reflected both Afro-American and Anglo-European fundaments. Formally, blues evolved from West African-derived field hollers, characterized by call-and-response vocalizing with improvised percussive rhythms and improvised choral polyphony, and from more European notions of harmonics and meter. Further, as Leroi Jones wrote in *Blues People,* "The whole concept of the *solo,* of a man singing or playing by himself, was relatively unknown in Western African music."[12] And Greil Marcus's essay on Robert Johnson in *Mystery Train* traces many of

the characteristic lyric obsessions of the blues to Puritan notions of sin and salvation.

Gospel, one of the richest and most neglected bodies of
American music, had similarly complex roots. It combined
African rhythms and call-and-response vocal patterns with a
broad range of European—and frontier American—influences. As gospel scholar Tony Heilbut wrote, "The first songs
slaves sang on this continent were probably those sturdy eigh-
teenth-century English hymns depicting amazing grace, Jordan's stormy banks, and fountains filled with blood." [13] By the
early 1800s, blacks were exposed to the camp meeting movement, a rural southern phenomenon whose highly emotional
tenor and rousing spiritual singing proved a profound influence. As was true of blues, gospel also assimilated European
ideas of harmonics and structure. Likewise, ragtime and the
other early intimations of jazz were formed from Afro-American approaches to rhythm, and European notions of formal
structure and instrumentation.

And though many white Southerners would recoil at the
thought, country music had its share of black influences. Early
country and blues featured variations on many of the same
songs, and country vocal styles leaned heavily on the blues.
This is due partly to the mammoth influence of Jimmie Rodgers, whose attention to blues stylings is obvious from nearly
all his recordings, but the debt doesn't end there. As country
music historian Bill C. Malone has pointed out, the blues was
also the source of such country rhythms as eight-to-the-bar
and rag, as well as some of its instrumental techniques: "Primarily through the influence of the Negro, the guitar came to
be more than a simple accompanying instrument; it came to
be a device for punctuating the moods and sentiments expressed . . . in effect, serving as a second voice." [14]

The genealogy of the Appalachian fiddle and banjo style
symbolizes this musical landscape. Brought to America by
white Europeans, the fiddle was for a time used primarily by
blacks, who played it at white social events. Eventually, it

was embraced by poor whites from the mountain country, who in turn absorbed black playing styles. And the five-string banjo, whose association with hill-country folk music and later bluegrass styles makes it seem an eminently white instrument, evolved from the bania, an African four-string antecedent.

If such a tangled lineage seems reminiscent of the "Hound Dog" story cited earlier, the history of minstrelsy, in its own grisly way, is even more so. Blackface minstrel shows featuring white performers arose in the 1830s as an extension of European musical theater, and—contrary to legend—bore no resemblance to the black musical styles of the day. After the Civil War, though, *black* minstrel groups began to pop up. The earliest, the Georgia Minstrels, appeared in 1865. Ten years later, the Fisk Jubilee Singers emerged. These groups retained many of the repugnant racial caricatures of earlier white minstrels (though in the process they at least introduced white audiences to the black music of the day). So latter-day minstrelsy amounted to black appropriation of a white form originally performed in blackface.

The motive force in nearly all these developments was black music, but the particulars always involved both blacks and whites. This dialectical interplay flies in the face of conventional wisdom about the South; it's easier to understand historically when you realize that the Jim Crow system didn't take hold there until the twentieth century. During slavery and on through the rest of the nineteenth century, blacks and whites associated regularly as a matter of necessity. As T. McCants Stewarts, a northern black journalist who traveled the South in the 1880s (he is quoted extensively in C. Vann Woodward's *Strange Career of Jim Crow*) observed in a letter to his editors, "I think the whites of the South are really less afraid to [have] contact with colored people than the whites of the North." He went on to say he encountered far less discrimination on trains and in restaurants of the South than anywhere else. Even after the onset of Jim Crow—and contrary to the cherished beliefs of many northern intellectuals—there continued to be more interaction between blacks and whites in the South than in the North, particularly among poor people working side by side in menial jobs. Though the tone of that interaction was usually uneasy at best, it still had an impact, and that impact was intensified by the advent of radio and phonograph records, which made surreptitious cross-cultural forays between southern "hillbilly" and "race" music even more common.

That nexus is precisely where the Stax and Muscle Shoals crews came from, and they were far from the first. If racial barriers have always counted for a lot in the development of American popular music, they nonetheless counted for less in music than in any other facet of culture. Black and white progenitors of contemporary pop shared some remarkably similar life experiences, after all. As Dobie Gray, a singer who returned to his lifelong interest in country music in the mid-1980s and made two of the finest records to come out of Nashville in that time, once told me of his Texas hometown, "Being poor and having to support your family and plow your land, having to wait for the crops to come in and wait for the rain, having to think about frost and all that—when you've got that in common in a small community, it goes beyond color." Besides common experience, they also shared a characteristically working class determination to make the most of the materials they found at hand—and they often found the same ones. When the Hawaiian style of guitar playing reached the South in the 1890s, for instance, blacks and whites alike seized on it, adapting from it the blues slide guitar technique and the pedal steel guitar, respectively.

That their explorations had much in common is best illustrated by the anomalies scattered through history: DeFord Bailey, a black harmonica player who in 1926 became the first featured performer on the Grand Ole Opry; Dock Boggs, a white blues singer from the same era; Jimmie Rodgers and Louis Armstrong's "Blue Yodel # 9" (1930), perhaps the first recorded interracial collaboration; and Ray Charles, who recorded two albums of country standards imbued with as much confidence and empathy as his gospel-derived R&B hits. In a sense you can locate the whole story of indigenous American music in the space between a black country singer like O. B. McClinton and a white R&B singer like Delbert McClinton. Or at Hank Williams's funeral in the Montgomery, Alabama Municipal Auditorium, where the entire balcony of the segregated theater was filled with black mourners, and the service was punctuated by the hymns of the Southwind Singers—a black gospel quartet.

The interracial complexity of pop music's roots defies the black nationalist vision of culture, which dictates that black culture has thrived not despite blacks' institutional separation from dominant society, but because of it. To the nationalist, a separate black community with its own economic infrastructure is a necessary precondition of black culture. And though this can make for strange bedfellows aesthetically—Nelson George has championed derivative white rappers the Beastie Boys on the grounds that they contribute to the cause by recording for black-controlled Def Jam—it's hardly surprising, since nationalists almost always elevate economics over the music itself. In the terms of an old proverb, nationalists locate the cultural significance of black music in neither the singer nor the song, but in the publishing company.

It isn't difficult to see why the black professional and entrepreneurial class might embrace this view, but it inverts the real significance black music has for most of its consumers, black and white. For them, the greatest impact is right there in the grooves, not in the means by which the music is produced. (Nor is that impact just aesthetic: It's not entirely coincidental that the civil rights movement gained its greatest white support in the 1960s, the decade following the infusion of black culture into white households through rock 'n' roll and R&B.) Besides, it's impossible to claim that an economically separatist black community is a precondition to powerful black music. History doesn't bear it out, and neither does the contemporary Minneapolis scene, which has become a focal point of black pop in the late eighties.

One way to understand Minneapolis is by contrast to Detroit, the most far-ranging and influential northern center of black pop since World War II. The source of Detroit's musical strength lay in its large and varied black population, much of which migrated en masse from the rural South during and after the war. These people brought with them a set of established musical traditions, and they settled by necessity into poor, mostly segregated neighborhoods, which ensured that those traditions would take root; consequently, it's possible to follow the development of the blues and R&B in a relatively straight line from the acoustic blues of the Mississippi Delta to the electrified music that later took shape in cities such as Detroit and Chicago. Moreover, Detroit blacks were a diverse enough group to encompass not only blues and R&B; there was also a nascent middle class to support the growth of jazz, which was actually the young Berry Gordy's first love.

Minneapolis could hardly be more different. Never exactly a center of heavy industry, it didn't offer migrating blacks the same opportunities as other major northern cities. As of the 1980 census, blacks constituted roughly 2.4 percent of the Minneapolis–St. Paul metro area population; despite the presence of a few ethnic enclaves (most notably, Irish and Slavic) in St. Paul and on Minneapolis's north side, the predominance of German and Nordic elements may well make it the most homogeneous major urban area in the country. If Prince's racially and sexually mixed bands have given some people the impression that Minneapolis is an integrationist mecca, it's important to remember some of the city's *other* prominent exports, including the Twins, an organization that continually vies with the Mets and the Red Sox for the title of whitest team in baseball, and the ultrawhite pastoral fantasies of Garrison Keillor's *Prairie Home Companion.*

Besides their small numbers, the blacks who do live in the area didn't move there in the same concentrated influx as in Detroit, which has made for a less pronounced black culture. Nor do most of them have any direct connection to the southern heritage that produced most of the major movements in earlier black pop. By the 1980s, almost all the local black musicians were Midwest born and bred: Jesse Johnson grew up in Rock Island, Illinois, where he came of age playing Led Zeppelin covers in a biker bar; Morris Day likewise moved to Minneapolis from a small city in Illinois. Terry Lewis spent his early years in Omaha before his family moved north; Prince and Jimmy (Jam) Harris were born in Minneapolis. Of the major talents to emerge from the city in the eighties, only Alexander O'Neal—born in Natchez, Mississippi—had extensive roots in southern R&B.

This is not to suggest there was no black music happening in Minneapolis before the 1980s explosion; critic David Adams has sketched the historical outlines in his "Roots of a Revolution" essay. But the musical movers of the eighties were less influenced by their local antecedents than by what they heard on radios and turntables, and that was a mixed lot indeed. Prince once told an interviewer he heard more country music as a child than any other kind, and a friend of mine who clerked at a downtown record shop in the early eighties confirms the tales of his eclecticism. Prince, he says, would pop up at the shop every couple of weeks, and might buy anything from James Brown to Dolly Parton to Molly Hatchet. By this time, of course, Prince could finally afford all the records he wanted, but tastes as catholic as his weren't uncommon among young blacks in Minneapolis, and they resulted from practical considerations more than ideological choices. As Terry Lewis put it, "To an extent, the music we're making today is the result of white rock 'n' roll radio and black music station static. None of *our* radio stations would come in as good as the mainstream stations. You could hear the beat and the rest was noise." (Ironically, this remark—made to writer

Martin Keller in 1984—prefigured the formula that gave Flyte Tyme Productions its first crossover blockbuster two years later in Janet Jackson's *Control,* a wedding of accessible pop melodies and funky electronic beats.)

What all these men share is a disrespect for the lines drawn by white racists and black separatists alike. As Lewis's observation implies, this attitude was born of need; the only culture available to them was a polyglot mass culture. But it also expresses the enormous ambition of talented young men and women—ambition shaped in an environment where the very idea of succeeding meant reaching outside the black community as they knew it. In Minneapolis, owing to the small black population and to a goodly dollop of genteel northern racism, black culture has always been all-but-invisible from the outside: There were never more than two or three local clubs where black musicians could play. (That's one reason the *studio* is the preferred metier of nearly every black act that's emerged from there.) And so, said Jimmy Jam, "Black musicians were going, 'We can't get a job; we better make a demo tape or something and try to get up out of here.' Prince did it; Rocky Robbins [one of the first major label signees from the city] did it. That's why *we* made it out here. Not that we had more talent [than the white musicians]; nothing like that. We just had more initiative, because there was nothing here for us."

According to the terms of black nationalist ideology, the Minneapolis scene ought to have been impossible in the first place; instead, it became a germinating center of pop music in the eighties. Its achievement hasn't been a triumph over assimilationism, as some critics insist that black music should be, but a triumph of integrationist impulses. The best Minneapolis has had to offer—*Dirty Mind, Purple Rain* (the album), *Sign of the Times* (album and movie), *Control,* Alexander O'Neal's excellent Flyte Tyme-produced albums, the Time albums, Jesse Johnson's *Shockadelica*—mixes up funk, rock, soul, jazz, and high-tech adventurism, skewing musical categories with a self-assurance and accessibility more and more at odds with pop music's growing fragmentation.

But being a successful black person in a racist society can hardly fail to have its complications. Of the Minneapolis musicians, Prince especially has been singled out by critics of crossover, who wax contemptuous over his exotic clothing and imagery, his ambiguous sexuality, and the advantages he derives from having light skin. There is no doubt that these factors have made it easier for Prince to cross over than, say, Alexander O'Neal, a man who is bigger, darker, and more unmistakably heterosexual; but to scrutinize Prince rather than the society that raises the barriers he got around is just another way of blaming the victim, and to presume (as the separatist ideologue almost always does) that O'Neal's expression of blackness is more "authentic" than Prince's is an awfully monolithic and condescending view of what it means to be black.

Terence Trent D'Arby, the most outspoken and talented new black artist to surface in the late 1980s, has blasted his contemporaries for pulling punches:

**Black male acts are far, far too apologetic. . . . Look, any black act in the States who has been [a] massive quote-unquote crossover success has had to emasculate himself to some degree. Prince has had to play the bisexual image, cast aspersions as to his dominant heterosexuality, Jackson's had to be asexual, Vandross couldn't possibly offend anybody, George Benson . . . it's like in the contract, it certifies them to a free plastic surgeon visitation, guarantees them a makeup artist at all times to lighten 'em up for photographs if you sell more than two million albums, and these guys wouldn't do or say anything which would lose them one record sale.[15]**

D'Arby obviously abhors these perceived accommodations to the dominant society, and that may be why he neglects to mention his own: He, like Jimi Hendrix before him, moved to Britain (where the racial equation is different, at least for American blacks) to launch his career.

What's disturbing about the whole notion of compromising, of making accommodations, is not compromise itself, but the implication—dating all the way from 19th-century black minstrelsy to Michael Jackson's multiple nose jobs—that the compromises are motivated by racial self-hatred. This specter has haunted the whole history of integrationism, most pointedly in the entertainment field; it figures in Prince's bizarre 1986 film, *Under the Cherry Moon,* whose subtext is really the psychology of crossover.

*Cherry Moon* is ostensibly the story of Christopher Tracy (Prince), a gaudily dressed piano bar gigolo on the French Riviera, and his sidekick Tricky (Jerome Benton). They work the Côte d'Azur's rich white women for fun and profit until Christopher falls for Mary Sharon, the daughter of an overbearing shipping magnate who is equal parts Darth Vader and Colonel Klink. Theirs is a star-crossed romance in the worst Hollywood tradition; before he dies in Mary Sharon's arms under the cherry moon, shot by her father's toadies and with blood already congealing on his lip, Christopher winsomely observes, "We had fun, didn't we?"

As drama, *Cherry Moon* was rightly panned; I remember walking out of the theater on opening night feeling an acute sense of embarrassment for Prince, who seemed to have poured his heart and soul into this ill-conceived, badly-made . . . what? Screwball melodrama? But if it's easy to see what makes *Cherry Moon* so awful, it's harder to see what makes it so *weird.* Like every major Prince project between 1980–86, *Cherry Moon* is partly an extension of its maker's own self-mythology. These myths have always been tailored for public consumption, but they also help, I think, to explain Prince to Prince. So it's not surprising that under all the dreck, the movie does lay claim to a vision. And though it makes little sense as dramatic narrative, it has considerable resonance as psychodrama.

Symbolically, *Cherry Moon* is an exercise in world-making. How is this world different? It's immediately striking that although Christopher and Tricky are practically the only blacks around, and outlandishly dressed to boot, their presence at teas and garden parties on the Riviera commands no special attention; the whole environment is characterized by a colorblindness that looks genuinely surreal to American eyes. When Tricky starts a funky dance line with the guests at Mary's birthday party, portly bejeweled matrons join in without question, as though they do this sort of thing all the time. And Mary's father, an ogre of the first order, never even alludes to Christopher's blackness in protesting their romance. It's clear enough that Chris and Tricky belong to a different class—they're gigolos, bon vivants—but the allusions to skin color are few and far between. In adjudging their respective appeal to Mary, Christopher boasts that he's "butterscotch" to Tricky's "chocolate," and at one point Christopher does use the word "black" in speculating what Mary would sound like when she fucked.

But that's about it. *Cherry Moon* is Prince's rendering of a world in which the barriers he must confront (or finesse) as an American black man simply don't exist. Christopher and Tricky are rogues, to be sure, but they aren't debarred by color. In this sense the movie offers a fantasy not unlike that suggested by Michael Jackson's long-form "Bad" video, in which the aspiration is neither to be black in any traditional sense nor to pass for white; it is to become a new class of being altogether: free, mobile, empowered, colorblind—the "new breed" Prince used to exalt in the days when he intentionally obscured his own racial origins (claiming falsely that his mother was white) and heterosexuality (singing songs like "Jack U Off"). Christopher embodies the bohemian's contempt for social conventions, but he is also full of the working class kid's hunger for middle-class legitimacy. So he is forever standing outside, while part of him proclaims his own superiority and part of him *just wants in*. (This tension between breaking rules and craving legitimacy has been evident throughout Prince's own career; in fact, *Cherry Moon's* soundtrack album, *Parade*, was disappointing precisely for its abandonment of visionary rock and funk fusions in favor of more "serious" art-rock posing.)

*Cherry Moon* may begin in a utopia where contradictions of race and class are at least superficially settled—if only by Christopher's insistence that he's *above* them—but in Prince's fantasyland (unlike Jackson's), the dark currents of reality keep lapping at the shore. However easy Christopher may find it to mingle at soirees, he *does* die in the end for his ambitions; then and only then does the movie tacitly own up to the weight of the taboos it has so blithely ignored. Christopher becomes a martyr to his crossover dreams, leaving Tricky to live out those dreams. With a bankroll from the grieving Mary, he moves back to America and buys a swanky highrise apartment building in Miami.

Many blacks felt betrayed by the film, and it's not hard to see why. It incessantly equates elegance and desirability with white skin; in its most disturbing moment, after Christopher has seemingly lost Mary and launched himself on a long drunk, he is galvanized back into action by the appearance of a heavy, buck-toothed black woman who asks in grotesquely coquettish tones when he'll "visit" her again. No amount of rationalization can undo the violence of that moment, but it's important to understand it in the broader context of Prince's career. With the possible exception of the *Cherry Moon* soundtrack, it's impossible to charge that Prince has tried to distance himself from his blackness or from black musical tradition; the delightful *Sign of the Times* concert movie (1987) was in fact the hardest shot of funk he'd yet delivered.

What Christopher runs from is not just a black woman, but a symbolic reminder of a heritage of limits, of powerlessness. That doesn't make his gesture any less odious, but it does highlight an intellectual bind racism creates for ambitious blacks. In America, It's an article of faith that each person has a right to advancement, a right to fashion his or her own destiny (and, hence, identity) without reference to the past. It's the stuff that Fitzgerald's *The Great Gatsby* and Faulkner's *Absalom, Absalom!*—arguably the two best American novels of the century—are made of. And never mind that, like Christopher, Jay Gatsby and Thomas Sutpen are ultimately killed by their visions; self-creation remains one of the most cherished myths of American life. The heart of *Cherry Moon*, the source of its willful colorblindness, is Christopher/Prince's assertion of the right to define himself in terms that completely override race. Prince has worked at something similar his whole career, but always with a handicap: Whereas David Bowie's wardrobe of identities earns him at worst the labels of poseur and dilettante, Prince's earn him epithets of racial treason.

If *Under the Cherry Moon* carries the crossover impulse too far, to the point where it begins to be a denial of blackness itself, it is hardly more errant than the black nationalist rhetoric that stands as its counterpoint in a polarized racial climate—a rhetoric which, as Ralph Ellison pointed out, presumes that blacks alone among all the American peoples "remain unaffected by the climate, the weather, the political circumstances—from which not even slaves were exempt— the social structures, the national manners, the modes of production and the tides of the market, the national ideals, the conflicts of values, the rising and falling of national morale, or the complex give and take of acculturalization which was undergone by all others who found their existence [in America]." These remarks appeared in Ellison's review of Leroi Jones's *Blues People*, an ambitious and temperamentally separatist treatise on black music; of its author, Ellison continued, "Jones has stumbled over that ironic obstacle which lies in the path of any who would fashion a theory of American Negro culture while ignoring the intricate network of connections which binds Negroes to the larger society. To do so is to attempt a delicate brain surgery with a switchblade."[16]

However bogged down the struggle for integration has become in the twenty-five years since Ellison wrote those words, popular music is still in the vanguard. By any reasonable measure, black music continues to be underrepresented on pop charts and CHR radio; nonetheless, it presents black people and black art on a larger scale and in more humanizing terms than any other facet of mass culture. The popularity of black music also exposes to anyone with eyes and ears just how profoundly black experience has shaped the cultural mainstream. To deny blacks their rightful place in the heart of American culture is not only a gross political injustice, but a denial of reality which, so long as it prevails, makes it impossible for *anyone* to understand the lifeblood of the culture.

# Picking up
# the pieces

V
I
D
E
O

P
O
P

## THE BIG SELL

In the glory days of the record business—the mid-1970s, when everyone assumed that sales would just go up and up—being a rock critic was like being the object of a demented charity. I'm not just talking promotional posters and T-shirts here. Records came then with solid goods: brief cases, jars of marmalade, a road map of the British Isles, a clock, playing cards, an in-car vacuum cleaner. It was if record companies could only guarantee the value of their own fleeting products by associating them with something *really* useful. W. F. Haug[1] has described the similar use of free gifts in the wooing of the public by high art manufacturers: collect the complete works of Wagner and get a bath towel free!

These days rock's usefulness is signaled in other ways. In just one day's mail in 1987 I got the WEA reissue of The Newbeats' 1962 "Bread and Butter," stamped now with the Little Chef

logo (it's the song of the television ad campaign for the restaurant chain), Jive's *Magic* dance track anthology packaged
with the new Adidas sports top and shoe catalog, and a press
release from Motown announcing that Smokey Robinson's
"The Tracks of My Tears," originally recorded in 1965, "is
heavily featured in the Oscar-winning film *Platoon,* which is
the current British number one box office success." The song
has "also been chosen by Budweiser for use in their new TV
campaign."

The use of classic rock, soul, and even blues songs as commercial backing tracks (musical highpoint so far: Otis Rush's
"So Many Roads" used to sell Vauxhall cars) is so familiar
now that the only time I'm jolted is when I realize how *organized* the process has become. Take this March 1987 advertisement from *Creative Review* (a journal for British ad
agencies), the copy arranged around a Grace Jones shot:

**SBK Songs now have the rights to the entire CBS Songs
catalogue. That's over 150,000 titles available for use in
advertising. Anything from Lennon and McCartney to the
Wombles. There's no middleman. We work directly with
your agency, quickly and efficiently. David Robson is the
man to talk to, and you won't have to break down his
door to see him. If it's an SBK Songs title, he'll get back to
you with a figure and a copy of the song the very next
day. No more slave to the rhythm.**

Such deals are profitable all around. Record companies and
song publishers get a new way of exploiting their back catalog and, while it is certainly more expensive for advertisers to
use established hits rather than to record new music of their
own, familiar songs ensure audience attention. As Gerry
Moira of the McCormick agency asks, "Why not buy tunes that
millions of people paid good money to send soaring up the
charts?" Moira has successfully sold Renault cars with

Cream's "I Feel Free," and Pirelli tires with the Doors' "Riders of the Storm."

What's striking about such advertisers' use of music is that the tracks they choose are those that were, as hits, the most "meaningful," in terms of youth culture, soul emotion, or "art." Most agencies don't use rock songs simply as a lazy way of reaching the "popular" audience; tracks are selected for *what* they stand for. Nike used the Beatles' "Revolution" to sell shoes, for example, because the song (or, rather, John Lennon's voice) meant an immediately sympathetic response to the sales pitch from the over-25 market. What's new about the rock/ad agency tie-in is not the exploitation of stars' selling power as such (Coca-Cola has been using rock and pop idols that way for at least thirty years) but the use of anticommercial icons to guarantee the "authenticity" of the product they're being used to sell. The most valuable rock sales figure in 1985–86 (apparently worth twelve million dollars to Chrysler) was, therefore, Bruce Springsteen, precisely because he famously refused all sponsorship or endorsement deals. Agencies were obliged to employ a series of *implied* Springsteens, aware of the paradox that if Bruce ever did agree to a commercial deal his stock on the ad market would fall immediately.

It's obviously galling for old rock stars (and fans) to find their heartfelt sixties songs selling suntan lotion and money services, but what interests me about this is not the ethical but the semiological implication. If rock songs and stars can be used so easily to signify "rock" during TV's commercial breaks, what does rock itself now mean? The answer is "the same as it ever did," but now in a context in which the old rock values—brash individualism, impatient community, youthful rebellion, and sensual delight—are played back as memories and longings that can only be reached by spending money on other goods. The advertisers don't just cynically manipulate the aging rock audience; the aging rock audience already believes it has lost its hold on the rock secret, which is why the advertisers' smooth promises touch us. Nostalgia and authenticity provide salespeople with such effective patter because we do believe that rock's aim was once true, our desires once unequivocal. And the more our memories are corrupted (putting John Lennon to work selling shoes, Jim Morrison selling tires) the more their account of the past becomes the measure against which we judge the value of the present.

Think of it as the rock version of the postmodern condition: a media complex in which music only has meaning as long as it keeps circulating, "authentic" sounds are only recognized by their place in a system of signs, and rock history only matters as a resource for recurrent pastiche. This threatens the authority of rock musicians, critics, and fans alike. Success in the music business is no longer a reward for effort, no longer a measure of good taste or quality, but depends on a quite irrational process in which sounds and songs and performers are plucked from the margins by voracious sales media, packaged, sold, and tossed back to obscurity.

Take Ben E. King's "Stand By Me," the soul classic originally issued in 1961. In 1986 Levi's in Britain announced that the song would be featured in their forthcoming 501 jeans campaign. King's record company (aware of the sales success of previous Levi's soul tracks) instantly began their own video-supported sales campaign: "Stand By Me" was marketed with the slogan "as used in the Levi's commercial," and the song's R&B history (and King's own R&B status) was quite irrelevant to the track's subsequent British chart success. Meanwhile, back in the United States, the same track had turned up over the closing credits of the movie *Stand By Me,* for no good reason except the shared title. It was sufficient exposure to put the record back in demand by record shoppers and radio listeners, and WEA started a sales campaign here too: the American video featured King and the kids from the film. Who was selling what, who was hearing what, became more and more confused in both countries.

King hasn't had further chart success, of course. In this world of crossmedia tie-ins, pop emotion gets transferred from an unexpected personal response into the orchestrated sign of a lifestyle, and there's not much any individual musician can do to script their own star part. But "postmodernism" is not just some sort of *geist*, a cultural malaise to which all institutions and artists and audiences must adapt. It describes too the effect of *material* changes in the relations of cultural production. If the meaning of rock has changed, from youth counterculture to shopcounter culture, it is because of technological developments and demographic shifts. The point I want to make in this essay is that rock *can't*, any longer, mean what it used to (which is precisely why we're so attracted to those ads and films and videos in which it still does).

# BUSINESS PREMISES

The starting point for any understanding of the music business today must be the "crisis" that hit the industry in the late 1970s. After more than twenty years of steady growth (and a decade of *spectacular* growth—the value of worldwide record sales rose from $4.75 billion to $7 billion between 1973 and 1978), record companies found that sales had peaked and that their rock-oriented working practices (the signing of numerous acts, the huge investment in studio time, the optimistic expenditure on promotion) made increasingly less economic sense. The year of truth was 1978–79, when music sales fell by 11 percent in the United States (from $4.13 billion to $3.69 billion) and by 20 percent in Britain, but the decline continued until 1981–82. By 1983, figures were back at 1979 levels, but record sales remained erratic. Few record company bosses greet the occasional flurry of "the boom is back" stories with anything other than skepticism: the number of gold records each year has never reached its 1978 level, and it is now taken for granted that "recovery" has, in *Billboard*'s 1984 words, been "due more to the runaway success of a handful of smash hits than to an across-the-board pickup" in sales (the biggest of these smashes was Michael Jackson's *Thriller*: released at the end of 1982, five years later it had sold 38.5 million copies worldwide). Even in 1986, when money returns in both the United States and the U.K. were the highest ever (thanks largely to the market take-off of the relatively expensive compact disc) the number of *units* sold was still well below the 1978 level.

But while the "crisis" for record companies was real enough (the number of CBS employees worldwide fell from 17,160 in 1980 to 10,110 in 1986), it is futile to spend time wondering about what went wrong with musical "creativity" or audience expectations. If some record company executives blamed their troubles on the false promise of disco (1978 was the year of *Saturday Night Fever*) and all thought they had been laid low by hometaping, what we must remember is that record labels are only minor divisions of leisure corporations these days (and that's as true for independent leisure companies like Geffen, Chrysalis, or Virgin as for the multinationals like Polygram and CBS). There was a crisis of record company *profitability* in the late 1970s, but it was resolved less by the restoration of returns from record sales than by the flow of music business capital into new areas of money-making.

At the time, American record companies perceived their market problem as the new competition for the teenage dollar created by computer games, and WEA duly went into partnership for their production with Atari. British executives, however, noted the effect of videocassette recorders, which took off much faster there than in the United States. By 1984, 35 percent of British households had VCRs, domestic leisure equipment that no one had had in 1976. It's clear that what was going on was indeed a crucial change in the use of

television. Just as the original rise of TV as family entertainment in the 1950s led to the marketing of youth music and
youth radio (record makers and advertisers had to find new
specialist markets), so the deregulation of television, the
spread of new cable and satellite services, and the use of the
TV screen for video games and rented films, presented
the record industry with a new sort of competition for leisure
resources.

The competition that counts here is not for the consumer's
time and cash—record buying *versus* TV viewing—but for
investment capital. The reorganization of television means
new opportunities for musical profit; the returns from selling
sounds to the public are beginning to be matched by the
returns from selling musical entertainment to the media. Two
aspects of this are worth noting. First, the growth in demand
for programs simply to fill all the airtime now available gives
the music industry new, risk-free, sales opportunities. ("Long-
form" pop videos like concert footage or star biographies, for
example, are particularly attractive to satellite TV services because of their international appeal.) Thus a business that has
long been organized around the vagaries of public taste and
the problems of overproduction, now enjoys the benefits of
*preselling*: the programs are designed and sold to advertisers,
cable companies, and/or station programmers before they're
even made. Preselling, however, doesn't preclude the possibility of eventually selling to the public; the record industry is
expecting good things from compact disc videos, and most
companies are hoping to make their long-form videos do-
mestically popular, too. Virgin's "video biographies" series,
for example, was launched in autumn 1987 for private rather
than public consumption (first subjects: Rod Stewart, the Bee
Gees, Marc Bolan, Abba, and the Kinks.) Companies like Virgin, Geffen, and Island have moved into the film business
proper precisely because the market opened up by home
video purchase and rental is the one they already understand:
young, male, home based.

Second, specialist video-pop television services like MTV now exist in all major music markets. MTV was set up in exact imitation of Top 40 radio, and record companies first used it simply as a new form of promotion, supplying free clips funded from the artists' marketing budgets. MTV was particularly important in the United States because it offered, for the first time, a means of immediate national exposure and appeared just as commercial pop radio stations were being frozen into "classic" rock, album track, and oldie formats. TV promotion was a godsend to an industry struggling to break new acts to new audiences, desperate to increase the *velocity* of musical consumption. But the sheer cost of video promotion plus the continuing decline of record sales—particularly in the singles market—made the idea of video promoting every release increasingly irrational, and the use of TV began to change. In order to insure the sales to cover the video costs, record companies had to invest equally heavily in all the other aspects of promotion: packaging, print ads, touring, radio-wooing, etc. It has been calculated that a major campaign in the United States surrounding a single track, which may be being used to sell an album or to establish a star, is half-a-million dollars; in Britain the overall costs of even a routine pop promotion are around half-a-million pounds. The Pet Shop Boys, for example, reckoned to spend about £200,000 making their second LP, and budgeted £200,000 for the four video clips to accompany the singles that would be taken from it, and another "£200,000 for all the other promotional costs." The sales to justify all this—two million copies minimum—can only come from the international market.

Just as with long-form videos, the advantage of TV promotion—its use across national boundaries—is also a constraint: it only makes economic sense to fund video clips if they will be shown in all possible music markets. Such considerations have a determinate effect on record release and sales policies. As Human League's Phil Oakey explained when asked why the group released "I Need Your Loving," a flop single in Britain:

**Because of the cost of making videos, Virgin will not release different records in different territories. I knew "I Need Your Loving" was the next big record in America, it would go over well on their radio. So we had to say we wanted it out in Britain, otherwise we wouldn't get a video. If we don't get a video, we don't get a hit in America. I'm really annoyed about it because we had a run of about eleven Top 20 singles, which very few groups have had, and that's been broken by the failure of this single, which we knew would fail.**[2]

What Oakey is describing here is a music biz power structure in which performers and their fans are less important than TV programmers and advertisers. "Richard Branson's Virgin Group," noted a report in the *Observer*'s financial pages in early 1987, "already the owners of Music Box, the music service which now appears on Super Channel, is trying to spread his wings further in Europe. He is bidding to buy the French pop music TV station, TV6, along with CBS, and the record company Polygram." This bid failed but Virgin was clearly already thought of as an entertainment rather than a record company (and is now investing with the *Financial Times* and the retail clothes chain Next in a new European broadcasting satellite). Its profits may still be rooted in its ownership of musical rights, but these rights are no longer exploited only through the sale of discs.

Music television, in short, is not just a tool for selling records but also a means of making money out of musical properties directly. Video-pop channels now have to pay to use clips, whether through the exclusive use contracts negotiated between MTV and most large U.S. corporations, via the annual video license fee paid by the BBC, or in the play-for-pay deals done in the rest of Europe. The "promotional" clip has become a source of income in itself, perhaps a more important source of income, indeed, than the music it is supposedly selling. Record companies' "music" policy is increasingly determined by their understanding of the needs and possibilities of visual entertainment. As Island's Chris Blackwell remarks:

> **If you're in the entertainment business on the music side, you really need to be in films as well because I think they're really joining into one business. You need to have access to putting your music into other people's films, and expanding the horizons of your artists into scoring, performing, or having their songs in films. I also feel that one needs to be in the film business in order to understand it and have access to people who are good video makers.**[3]

As "one business" the music and film industries are locked into a mutually dependent relationship. On the one hand, Hollywood film sound tracks are now used routinely as record marketing tools; few singles top the charts in the U.S. these days that are not film-linked, and many British acts, like Simple Minds and Echo and the Bunnymen, have been dependent on teen-aimed movies for their initial exposure. On the other hand, the records are used to push the films; few hit films are released these days without an accompanying title song promotion.

The 1987 success *Dirty Dancing* (the story of a pre-Beatles vacation romance, produced by the home video company Vestron) exemplifies the way the film and music industries now work together. As Stephen Holden reported in the *New York Times*, Bob Fieden, "a pop talent scout and consultant to RCA records," was the first person to realize the script's sales potential.

> **"When I read it [said Fieden,] I saw something that had natural opportunities for music. It involved youth,**

dancing, and coming of age. I thought every teenage girl would identify with the Cinderella aspect of the story, and so I brought it to the attention of Bob Buziak, the president of RCA."[4]

Buziak was immediately interested:

"I had a lot of experience with sound tracks and seen what worked and what didn't. The movie *Back to the Future* grossed $150 million and had a No. 1 single with Huey Lewis; the soundtrack album only sold 600,000. That's because the music was "wallpapered" into the movie, and the songs were not an essential part of the emotional experience. For a soundtrack to be really successful—like *Top Gun* or *The Big Chill*—you have to hear what you see. And to make that happen, the director usually has to shoot scenes using either the actual music in the film or something that's very similar."[5]

Working in collaboration with Vestron's music consultant, record producer Jimmy Ienner, RCA put together both the movie and an album sound track. In Holden's words,

It was decided to intermingle the album's period music with its contemporary cuts in a way that no hit movie has done before. And where the film had used an 80 to 20 percent balance of old and new material, the soundtrack album would offer a 60 to 40 percent ratio of new to old.[6]

The *Dirty Dancing* strategy was not simply a matter of pro-motion—record to sell a film, film to sell a record. The strategy also determined *how* the film would be made in the first place and reflects the work popular music now has to do. This is the context in which rock has become, in Bill Graham's words, "the voice of corporate America"[7]—on advertisements, in

Hollywood blockbusters, as a prime-time TV score—it is no longer *directly* expressive of teen tastes.

The most obvious sign of the redistribution of music market power is the decline of the single. In 1986 in Britain, for example, for the first time since 1974, not one single release went platinum (sold a million copies), and overall singles' sales fell below seventy million for the first time since 1977 (twelve-inch versions, which accounted for about a third of these sales, could no longer be expected to stop the decline). In the United States, record companies have had to come to terms with a new youth market that may not even own a turntable, and neither cassette nor compact disc players are designed for single track play. (Compact disc singles are now marketed in Britain and the United States, but they were available only to radio stations for promotional purposes; even CDVs are expected to combine a video single with a sound album.)

In the rock business itself the single's economic rationale was always as a form of promotion and market research, a tool for selling an album and building a star. And as its promotional value increased in the late 1970s, (purchasers being wooed by all sorts of special offers: posters, remixes, etc.) so its own money-making importance declined. In the British industry, certainly, singles buyers were pursued in order to get a disc onto the charts and into clubs and therefore to guarantee airplay. It was the organization of radio and dance floor entertainment rather than the consumers' own demands that determined the stress on singles sales—other ways of selling LPs, via TV advertising, for example, were much more expensive and inflexible. The point, though, was that even if the single was being used only as a means of LP and star promotion, it gave a place at the heart of the profit-making machine to the most volatile sector of pop taste— young people, with their more or less unpredictable response to an immediate sound in their lives.

By the late 1980s this situation had subtly changed. Singles are still vital promotional tools (MTV is organized around the clip like radio is organized around the track), but their effectiveness is no longer directly dependent on teen choice. Instead that effectiveness is determined by the readings of teen (and other audience) tastes taken by TV and film companies that are, for technological reasons, much less responsive to youth cultural fads and fashions than pop radio used to be. The point is not that the record industry has to reach its market *through* other entertainment media (this has always been true), but that its profits now depend on its delivery of that market *to* those media. A record company's most rewarding economic role has become selling audiences to advertisers, programmers, and products.

This is reflected in the increasingly complex deals made by the music and advertising industries. In late 1986 *Rolling Stone* launched *Marketing Through Music,* "a monthly newsletter," in Leslie Savan's words, "written for ad folks and company execs, encouraging them to use rock stars to hawk their products."[8] This means not just endorsements, the mating of big stars and big products (Lionel Richie and Tina Turner, or Michael Jackson and David Bowie getting 6- and 7-figure dollar sums to promote Coke and Pepsi), but also sponsorship, corporate investment in all aspects of the rock process, from garage to stadium. Sponsors are not just concerned to hang their names on already glamorous or famous figures—presenting Sting or the Stones, for example; they can become equally involved in star-making, thus proving their genuine commitment to rock culture and tying its very "risks" to a product's image.

Coors, notes Savan, keen to woo the young audience and counter its bad political image, is on the lookout for "up-and-coming new music groups in New York." In Britain, Harp Lager sponsors the Institute of Contemporary Art's rock weeks, showcases for new and radical acts, where people who appreciate interesting music can get together and drink an interesting beer. In Scotland, McEwan's lager deliberately chose unknown bands and unknown songs for its 1986 TV ads. The sales target were 18-to-24-year-olds who were taken to be "much more sophisticated than before, far more lifestyle and image conscious, far more trendy. We just cannot afford to insult or patronize this new public."[9] And McEwan's made sure they got lots of coverage for their support of the young Scottish pop scene. (What the company did not publicize was that one of their young groups, Win, had to rerecord their song, "You've Got the Power." Under British TV regulations beer must not be associated by advertisers with macho values. "Power," an unacceptable keyword, had to be changed to "tower"!)

The subordination of popular music policy to corporate need was anticipated in the mid-1970s by Rockbill, a company designed to match rock acts and corporate sponsors in the organization of live music. Most rock tours, like most rock singles, had long made economic sense only as means of promotion, and so contributions to their costs were gratefully received by performers' managements and record labels. From their perspective there didn't seem to be much difference between selling advertising space in the concert program to selling it on the stage, and few groups tour extensively without a sponsor now (and those that do—like Springsteen and Prince—have turned down million dollar offers).

As such "innocent" sponsorship deals became a part of record companies' financial calculations (like video costs and film sound-track opportunities) so would-be recording groups began to be assessed for their corporate potential: "Is there a sponsor for them?" became as important a question as "is there a market for them?" And sponsors are, on the whole, more conservative than consumers, and more likely to be prejudiced about black music, female musicianship, and *difficult* groups generally (in marketing terms, being difficult is certainly not the same thing as being interesting). The apparent paradox here—companies buy stars because they stand for a rugged independence (like ZZ Top) or artistic integrity (like David Bowie) that is then compromised by being bought—is resolved by the advertisers' visual stylization of rock. Sound and image swirl in perfect understanding, and all that's going to be consumed, at last, is the beer, the jeans, the running shoes. The musician is just there as a sign of lifestyle. In the ideal world of sponsorship the meaning of the music and the product is the same; the performers' public appeal, their cultural value, is guaranteed by the sponsors, just as the sponsors' cultural value is guaranteed by the stars.

As Leslie Savan notes, one reason why rock stars are such successful salespeople is their expertise in selling themselves.[10] Sales of star "merchandise" long predated sponsorship as a way of covering tour losses. At all big shows we now take for granted the "official" program and T-shirt stalls, the "official" hawkers of scarves, posters, and shoulder bags. British groups like Duran Duran made their biggest touring profits from merchandise not ticket sales, and Dave Marsh notes that Bruce Springsteen's *Born in the U.S.A.* tour was "unquestionably the single largest merchandise-grossing tour in the history of rock and roll"[11] (according to Bill Graham, co-owner, with CBS, of Winterland, the company that did Springsteen's merchandising for him, selling goods from buttons to sweat shirts at $22). It's not surprising that chain record stores now have racks of official T-shirts as extensive as their racks of tapes and records.

For anyone, like me, who came of age as a rock fan in the 1960s, record stores became, indeed, disconcerting in the 1980s. As the space for video and cassette tapes, star merchandise, and computer games expanded, so vinyl records themselves—simply as material goods—seemed to lose their place. And this process is now being completed by the rise of the compact disc. In a report on the music industry in mid-June 1987 the *Financial Times* suggested that the compact disc "saved" the U.S. music industry in two ways: it revived consumer interest in music, and it allowed companies to push the price of their product through the $10/£10 barrier. CD consumption took off in 1985, and in 1986 the sale of 53 million CDs generated almost as much income ($930 million) as the

125 million LPs sold ($983 million). In Britain the story was much the same (although there it wasn't until 1986 that pre-recorded cassette sales overtook those of albums). In both countries it is also clear that CDs reach "an older demographic" than LPs, and that their relatively higher cost of unit production entails tighter market control. (Record companies can't carry as many flop CDs as they can flop records; it's not surprising therefore that back catalogs have so far accounted for about ninety percent of CD sales.)

Chris Blackwell suggests that, in fact, the CD meant a return to the "quality" product (and the quality market) that had been neglected in the cost/price cutting policies of the late 1970s and undermined by the rise of the cassette, a "paperback" product in his terms.[12] The cassette plus the compact disc thus make much better sense of the taste division in the music market than the black vinyl alongside either. Tower Records' Russ Solomon agrees:

**What's going to phase out is a plastic thing with grooves in it. We're not selling records; we're selling programming material. We never sold records. We never sold tape. We never sold compact discs or videotapes. We only sell music and video programming. And it doesn't make a damn bit of difference whether records disappear. . . . Kids who are twelve years old today or younger, who are going to be our marketplace in just a few years, they don't have any romance with records. They have a romance with a tape. Or a romance with a CD or a video of some sort. They're going to need the video component or they're not going to understand the damn music.[13]**

If the CD saved the music business, then, it did so as part of its transformation. Until the late 1970s the organization of the world record industry hadn't changed much in principle since the days when Edison did international patent deals and EMI built record manufacturing plants across the Commonwealth. Multinational control of the hardware of record making and playing involved locally produced software, the sounds to suit local taste. Now, when Japanese companies control the hardware, the old Western music giants are, by necessity, in the business of selling their *sounds* across the world, and multinational corporate structures are getting ever more elaborate as a result. Thus the largest French record company, Ariola, is owned by the German-based publishing group, Bertelsman (which bought RCA's music division from General Electric); the once major British company Decca is now a minor subsidiary of the German-Dutch electronics and entertainment group Polygram; and the best-known American record label, CBS, is controlled by the Japanese Sony.

World superstars like the Beatles and Elvis Presley are no longer exceptional; every act signed up by a major company is expected to have worldwide appeal and is marketed accordingly (British record executives, for example, now assume that they won't make profits on their acts from their British sales). If one aspect of this is the development of music television crossing national broadcasting borders, another is the rise of the international record retail chain. Virgin has branches of its stores all across Europe; there are Tower Record stores in Britain and Japan as well as the U.S.A. On music television programs and in all these stores (as well as those of local rivals) exactly the same songs, stars, and discs are on display. In 1985, U.S. pop and rock stars sang "We Are the World" for famine relief; what was meant as statement of humility came out as a simple boast.

# STRUCTURAL IMPLICATIONS

**Within the music industry, songs are most frequently referred to by words depicting the stage in the decision process through which they are passing. Thus, a song is called "a copyright," "a property," "a demo," "a tape," "a**

dub," "a transcription," "a cut," "a master," "a side," "a release," "an A side," "a pick," "a selection," and finally "a hit" or "a dud." At all points in the decision chain, songs are regularly referred to as "product."

This distinctive product image nomenclature focuses the attention of creative people at each link in the chain on the commercial rather than on the aesthetic values of their work. "The point," one publisher told us, "is to make money, not art."

Having a product image is to shape a piece of work so that it is most likely to be accepted by decision makers at the next link in the chain. The most common way of doing this is to produce works that are much like the products that have most recently passed through all the links in the decision chain to become commercially successful.[14]

John Ryan and Richard Peterson are describing how the country music business works here, but their model is equally applicable to rock. There is a tendency among rock idealists to argue that popular music is somehow *more* commercial now than it used to be, but my argument is, rather, that the basis of its commerce has changed. To use Ryan and Peterson's terms, the "crisis" of 1979–83 was a crisis in "product image," and its resolution doesn't mean that rock is any more (or less) a product than it was before.

In the music industry itself, a song—the basic musical property—represents "a bundle of rights"; income from the song comes from the exploitation of those rights, and what happened in the 1980s was that some of these (the "secondary rights") became more profitable, others (the "primary rights") less so. Thus songs may now be exploited more fruitfully through the fees paid for their use on the movie and television screen than by being "carried" on a tape or disc sold to the public, while a company's stockpile of old material —the back catalog—may now be a more important form of musical capital than a roster of new acts.

One consequence of this is a new relationship between "major" and "independent" labels. In the common sense of rock history and sociology it is an article of faith that the greater the number of music-issuing companies, the better the music. This has been interpreted historically in cyclical terms: every now and then (usually because of market opportunities opened up by new media) there is a burst of independent musical activity, and the majors' pop market dominance is challenged (as by Sun records and rock 'n' roll in the 1950s, or by the Atlantic and Motown labels and soul in the 1960s). There follows a period of "recuperation"—the majors start to compete with the indies in the new media and market and have the resources to service them much more efficiently (Elvis became a superstar with RCA not Sun, Ray Charles with ABC not Atlantic). The indies are taken over (like Atlantic) or go bust (like Sun), and there is a new period of market stability and musical stagnation. The available sounds get more homogeneous as the new pop formula is refined, until, eventually, there is another burst of independent musical activity (like punk in the mid-1970s) to meet increasingly unsatisfied consumer demand.

It is not at all obvious, though, that this model makes sense of current trends. Nowadays, in Heikki Helman's words,

**the pattern is rather that the smaller companies offer a test market for the competition between the larger companies, through which these companies can outline their musical production. The smaller companies have gained a permanent and important though subordinate position in the music industry. The cycles have changed into symbiosis. The new state of competition has to some extent created a music culture richer in variations.**[15]

One example of such "symbiosis" is the emergence of independent record labels as specialist oldie outfits (like Rhino in the United States, and Demon/Edsel and Ace in Britain) making money from (and for) those parts of the majors' back catalogs that are not worth digitally remixing onto compact disc because sales won't cover costs. (By the end of the century such oldie-indies' importance—and profits—may well come from their being the last remaining source of black vinyl.)

These labels don't just see themselves as conserving music (or recycling it in commercials). "Our job is to start and follow trends, just as the majors do with new talent,"[16] says Charly's Bob Fisher. "The fashions change in reissues just as they do in new pop." Fisher believes that re-releases can "directly influence the music played in fashion-conscious clubs and, hence, the choice of material for new groups on the live circuit." Phonogram's Mark Cooper notes that "the reissue labels have created their own young audience with an appetite for the sounds of the past." And EMI's Tony Wadsworth adds that "dancing at the Wag to 'The Sidewinder' only starts them off looking at the Blue Note catalog. There's enough music in there to last a lifetime."

Here, then, the independent labels play their old role: they have more direct links with the hip part of the public than the majors, and they are quicker to spot, and stoke, a trend. But now the majors benefit directly from their success and can move in to exploit their publishing and other rights if any old act or number does take off.

Something of the same routinized relationship between the indies and the majors is evident now in the exploitation of new talent too, an effect, paradoxically, of the fact that the "indie" has become an ideological rather than a musical or market label. Indie groups, companies, stores, magazines, and radio stations are defined by their independence of the commercial mainstream. This means that to take over indie successes the major labels have to tread warily, even though to develop any sort of long-term musical career the indie acts themselves have to link up somehow with the big promoters and distributors. In a 1987 debate with In Tape's Jim Khambatta in the magazine of the British indies, *The Catalogue,*

Geoff Travis of Rough Trade (instigator of much of the strategy of the post-punk British indie scene) thus defended the deals he'd done in setting up the Blanco y Negro label with WEA and Blue Guitar with Chrysalis, while reaffirming his opposition to "the conservative corporate moguls," and his belief in an "alternative" system of record production. He explained

**I'm not weakening it by taking out the Mighty Lemon Drops, The Jesus and Mary Chain, The Shop Assistants. These bands weren't interested in staying inside the [independent] system on the terms that were being offered to them. It takes a lot of money to support a band, it takes a lot more to promote and record a potential chart record. . . . All I did was to divert some of my time and energy to continue working with these groups, whom I love. The money I got for doing this has been used to finance the recording and promoting of many Rough Trade projects.[17]**

Travis was writing from the perspective of someone who'd seen bands Rough Trade had initially developed (from Scritti Politti to the Smiths) poached by major labels as soon as their star quality became apparent—and these days the resources to realize pop stardom clearly are beyond Rough Trade's means. Administering the major's "indie" signings for them is therefore a more sensible policy financially (and as a matter of independent principle) than vainly attempting to compete with them.

In the past the importance of small labels (like Sun or Atlantic) was to nurture new tastes and markets on which the majors then moved in, offering the same sounds and services on a glitzier scale. Now the independent labels are important in terms of "product development": they find new acts and test market them, bring them to the point of success from which the majors' campaigns start. Indie labels and producers have thus replaced live promoters as talent spotters. Chris Blackwell has noted the difference between the music scene now and when he began Island as a 1960s independent label:

**[Then] bands used to go out and play, develop fans, then try to get a record contract. Nowadays people get a record contract, buy the instruments, make the record, and then have the videos force-fed to the media.**[18]

There are two points to make about this situation. First, as Will Straw has noted,[19] the 1980s marked a clear division between two marketing strategies that had to some extent been integrated in the rock era. On the one hand there is the long-term thinking of artists like Paul Simon and Kate Bush. Their personas, their *artistry*, is so well established as the basis of their sales appeal that they can take considerable time (three years and more these days) to make an LP that is then released with the full panoply of interviews, publicity, a world tour, accompanying single and videos, etc. On the other hand, there is the short-term approach of artists like Madonna and A-Ha, whose personas work as trademarks rather than as means of self-expression—each new release creates its own drama of fame, stardom, and sales; these dramas are then enacted in the stars' careers as a series of dazzling moments on stage and screen.

Over the years the long-term acts (Phil Collins, say) make the most money for their companies, but the short-term acts generate the most excitement and determine how the sales process generally works. The biggest sellers of all, like Michael Jackson, combine both strategies. And the problem for the majors is that inasmuch as they still develop new acts, they have to sell them the short-term pop way—there's no live circuit left for unknown groups to build up fans and credibility. This makes it hard for upcoming musicians to shift into long-term gear: there's nothing *underneath* the breathless surface for "committed" fans to latch on to. Chris Blackwell again:

When you see the band, if the band is strong, you can start a career. If you start your first record with a group and it's beautifully, perfectly produced, there hasn't really been a chance for people to develop a credibility for the actual band itself. They're buying a record more than the band. I think then a group almost has to recover from that. Frankie Goes to Hollywood is a classic example of this. Their first record is sensational. It's so good, but then there's a serious question as to how good the band is. The band then has to spend the next period of their time getting credibility as a band.[20]

This suggests how the major companies most commonly use the indies now, as labels that produce *credible* stars. (In 1986, EMI made a shameless bid to sign up Britain's most successful independent acts; the company successfully enticed the Smiths and Cabaret Voltaire, it failed to tempt New Order and Depeche Mode).

To summarize, then, the old model of the record business, in which major and independent labels compete in a cycle of diversity and standardized oligopoly, no longer fits. Independent labels today offer specialist consumer services to the music market as a whole, just as they did before the rise of rock. They provide a supply of oldies, reggae tracks, sound effects, etc. Or else they function as the industry's research and development department, bring new acts to the point where their success can be guaranteed. The business accommodation of indies and majors is, in turn, dependent on the fragmentation of pop taste. Music sales policy nowadays depends not on competition *within* a unified industry, but on the relationship between a corporate center (for the production of worldwide, multimedia entertainment) and a *periphery* of local music scenes (little labels, independent producers, etc.) taking advantage of electronic technology and the fall in the relative cost of record and tape production.

It used to be assumed that "center" and "periphery" (or mainstream and margins) were joined in struggle (as "authentic" musicians faced the temptation to "sell out"), but bridged by the career ladder (as musicians went from local to national to international success). This assumption no longer holds true. The Beatles' story—from Liverpool to world domination in a series of ever-ascending steps—is irrelevant both to prepackaged video stars whose worldwide domination is planned from the start (e.g. CBS's remodeled Michael Jackson in the early 1980s) and to cult figures who don't expect ever to dominate the world at all. In this respect the rock career is now just like a career in jazz and other "minority" musics, but I can best explain what I'm talking about pictorially.

The old model of the music career was based on a pyramid, which I'll call The Rock:

THE ROCK

SUPERSTARS

INTERNATIONAL TOURING

INTERNATIONAL HITS
INTERNATIONAL GATEKEEPERS

MAJOR TOURING
NATIONAL PROMOTERS
NATIONAL STARDOM

MAJOR RECORDING   A&R   NATIONAL PRESS
NATIONAL RADIO/TV   NATIONAL HITS

[INDIE] RECORDING   SMALL LABELS   LOCAL RADIO
REGIONAL SALES

REGIONAL LIVE   LOCAL PROMOTERS   LOCAL PRESS
REGIONAL BUZZ

LOCAL LIVE   CLUB/PUB OWNERS   LOCAL BUZZ

MUSICIANS

The dynamic here is a push from below, the ruling ideology is a Horatio Alger-type account of success being *earned* by hard work, determination, and skills *honed* in practice. The superstars' position at the top of the pyramid is justified because they have *paid their dues* on their way up it.

Each rung of the ladder represents a different set of gate-keepers, and a successful push past them depends on the combined impact of the musicians and their audiences. This establishes "community" as the elemental meaning of rock, the cultural charge that is then mediated by promoters, record companies, press, radio, etc. To put it another way: it is the collective power of their music that determines, in the last instance, how far a rock act can go. Public performance authenticates studio appeal and defines the ideal audience/musician relationship.

Musicians can only go up the ladder; success works ratchetlike because it is a rational reflection of musicians' ability and impact. Stardom in this model is permanent—the value of The Grateful Dead, say, can be precisely measured by the number of years in which they have nurtured and been nurtured by their fans.

This is an ideological account of success; it assumes the rock career process that was established in the late 1960s is *normal,* a model of "making it" against which other pop stories (the Monkees, for example) could be measured or measure themselves (the Sex Pistols, say) and be found wanting.

There are still careers that follow rock rules (U2 is the most recent example), but the 1980s reorganization of the music business and the video selling of "new pop" groups like Duran Duran has meant the rise of an alternative success story. The second model, the way careers work now, I'll call The Talent Pool:

The dynamic here comes from the center. There are no longer gatekeepers regulating the flow of stardom, but multinationals "fishing" for material, pulling ideas, sounds, styles, performers from the talent pool and dressing them up for worldwide consumption.

The process is, from both the musicians' and audience's point of view essentially *irrational*. Who gets selected for success seems a matter of chance and quirk, a lottery, and success itself is fragmented, unearned, impermanent. The "creative" role in this pop scheme is assigned to the *packagers*, to record producers, clothes designers, magazine editors, etc.; they are the "authors" of success, the intelligence of the system.

"Audience" now describes the group delivered to advertisers and the media *by* music; it exists as any sort of collectivity only in this act of collusion. To put this another way, community is now *defined* by style: performance/audience relationships exist only as they are mediated.

Rock is now just one genre among others; as a form of worldwide entertainment no one mode of music is any more or less significant than any other. In its own local or cult backwater, faith in "the rock" may continue (just as there are groups of musicians and fans still dedicated to the idea of folk, the blues, country music, and the polka). But rock can no longer make any hegemonic claims.

The above two charts are ideal types, but the implications of the move from the rock to the talent pool are worth examining in more detail with respect to three issues: music as property; music as sound; the music market.

# PROPERTY

**My vision of the future of the music industry is at once a most exciting prospect and a threat to creativity. This is because, within a few years, technology will have advanced to such a level that the average home will possess a digital high-definition large-screen television, connected to a home computer. Through an interactive (two-way) cable system, the viewer would also be linked to a central bank—a library as it were, of sound and audiovisual recordings.**

**By dialing up the appropriate catalogue number on his own computer, the viewer could then choose from the library any musical or audiovisual recording he wanted to see or hear. This would be received by his television in digital stereo sound and with high-definition image. Or, he could receive video games or even computer programmes, all downloaded from the central bank in the living room.**

**For those people who cannot afford such a system, there would also be shops without stock. These shops would be nothing more than copying outlets, using high-**

**speed duplicating machines linked by cable to a central bank. The customer's requirements would be copied onto tape or other blank support.**

**The combination of new technology and the central bank will drastically reduce the market for prerecorded programmes. The average consumer will have little need to buy audio or video products when access to a central bank will provide him with a complete range of material from records and films to video games and computer software. In other words, the sales and distribution system for prerecorded material, as we know it today, will no longer exist.**[21]

This is the view from within the record industry itself, from IFPI—the International Federation of Phonogram and Videogram Producers. Gillian Davies is drawing attention here to the legal implications of the death of black vinyl and the emergence of a new recording technology: on the one hand, "an unlimited opportunity for private copying and piracy"; on the other hand, the rise of satellite and cable transmission systems that are "to a large extent, *uncontrolled* methods of distributing recordings to the public."

Davies divides the first problem into two: piracy (unauthorized reproduction of audio and visual recordings for commercial use) and home taping (ditto, for private use). In straight commercial terms there's no doubt that piracy has so far been much more of a menace. The case against home taping, even after a decade of record company propaganda, remains unconvincing. The industry line used to be that blank tapes were *replacing* records, but this reading from sales statistics didn't really address the question of who was taping records and why. More systematic market research found that the same people were buying records and blank tapes, and, as Russ Solomon, owner of Tower Records suggested, even to treat a record and a taped copy of that record as market equivalents is misleading. Both have become necessary for music-oriented consumers.

> They [record companies] say, "Well, it would be better if we didn't have home taping." I'm not so sure it would be. Because if you didn't have the home-recording business, you wouldn't have Walkman machines. In other words, the tape technology that came out of the recording machine resulted in the portable playback machine and the automobile machine, which created an enormous market for us. I've never been sure that a record that is taped would have resulted in a sale. We had a line: "Blank taping is the Hamburger Helper of the music business." The record that you're taping is a record that you very well may have bought. You tape a copy for your car.[22]

And the increasing use of blank tapes has, in fact, been more than matched by the increasing popularity of prerecorded cassettes:

> A lot of people find it inconvenient and time-consuming to tape on a regular basis, so they end up taking the easy way out. They buy the tape. That's what seems to be happening. We're not selling a blank tape at the expense of selling a record.[23]

Solomon calculated that sales of blank tapes only constitute about 3 percent of his business, and added more pointedly that the record industry's antitape argument lost much of its power once its own fortunes revived. The mass marketing of cassette machines had certainly changed people's *use* of music—not least because it gives us the opportunity to program our own LPs. But in encouraging (and sustaining) consumers' musical interests through the recession, it had probably done no real harm to record industry profits at all.

Piracy, by contrast, is a major and ever-growing commercial threat. The development of a worldwide superstar system means not just new technological opportunities for piracy but, just as importantly, new incentives, as well. Pirating a Michael Jackson means selling not just illicit copies of his records, but second-hand versions of his video clips, "unauthorized" posters, bundles of "false" merchandise, and so on. Even by 1982 the piracy figures were daunting—66 percent of the Asian record and tape market, 30 percent in Africa and the Middle East, 21 percent in Latin America, and 11 percent in Canada and the United States. European figures were lower (3 percent in Britain), but only by dint of expensive and time-consuming legal and detective work.

It is clear from IFPI reports that in international terms piracy is the major threat to record company returns, and such theft is generally accepted by public opinion as wrong. Why, then, has the record industry so consistently confused this issue with the much less publicly convincing claim that home taping is theft too? One answer lies in its fear of the future: just as compact discs arrived to "save" the music business, for example, so did a supposed threat to their sales—digital audio tape and the possibility that consumers would now just rent CDs and make their own high-quality audio copies.) IFPI lobbied hard to compel DAT hardware manufacturers to incorporate Copycode into their equipment, a device to make CD copying impossible.

This campaign was bound to fail. It made nonsense of the domestic sales appeal of DAT equipment, and whatever official deals were made, Copycode-free equipment and/or counter-Copycode devices would be for sale. The record industry knew this perfectly well, too, and it seems clear that the real point of the anti-DAT campaign was not to prevent copying but to get control of it, in both financial and legal terms. The sales levy imposed on blank tape and/or taping equipment in most European countries is, therefore, not just a source of additional income but functions more importantly as a license: people's "right" to home tape has to be paid for. (A sales levy is unlikely to ever be considered seriously in the United States; Britain's Conservative government changed its mind several times before deciding against it.) The point of this essentially ideological surcharge is not really to change domestic users' understanding of what they do (people will continue to assume that once they've bought a record they can do with it what they like), but to get governments to protect the record industry from the "uncontrolled use" (IFPI's words) of their product by anyone.

It is worth noting, in this context, that new technology is equally a threat to the control of music in noncapitalist countries. In East Germany, for example, the usual methods of restricting the import of Western sounds and the circulation of unofficial Eastern ones have completely collapsed under the impact of tape technology—and 'pirate' tapes and records in the Eastern block are obviously a Good Thing. Why not in the West too?

As if this were indeed the implicit question, the record companies' campaign for copyright reform stresses that under capitalist conditions market "control" of musical properties is what inspires "creativity" in the first place. As Gillian Davies of IFPI puts it:

**Governments must be convinced of the need to update and develop national copyright legislation to keep pace with new technology and to give adequate protection to rights owners in the light of all new uses of their creations.**[24]

Convincing governments (or public opinion) means convincing them of the justice (rather than straight self-interest) of the industry's cause. In Britain, at least, the "respectability" of the rock business as "a service industry for charities" like Band Aid and the Prince's Trust undoubtedly led to the government's 1985–86 support for a blank tape levy. Rhetorically ("home taping is theft"), record companies pulled the necessary trick: they defended their ownership of musical goods in terms of artistic integrity, riding on the musicians' coattails as equal "creators," the people who *realized* the musicians' dreams. This was to peddle a nineteenth century, Romantic view of art. Pieces of music—"works"—belong to artists. Their labor and talent is embedded in them and we, as consumers, should pay accordingly for the right to use and enjoy them. Record companies are the media for this exchange.

This may be a reductive account of how pop actually works as a commodity, but this structure is built into the sales system. We think in terms of a Bruce Springsteen or Madonna record; only retailers and distributors talk more accurately of a CBS or a WEA LP. It is this sytem which is threatened by new technology. The debates about taping and copying may focus on what is meant by a musical property, but what is really at issue is what is meant by music.

## S O U N D

**Right now it's fascinating to me. This is the most stimulated I've ever been in my whole life. I can't even keep up with all this junk I'm buying. To me the most fascinating thing, and I know to some people this is going to sound like a drag. . . . We're working out systems where if somebody who lives in England, say, has a system similar to what I have, and he's got a track and he wants me to play on it, well, he can send it to me over the satellite to New York. My system can then pick it up. It will go down on tape. I can listen to it, put my guitar overdub on it, send it back to him, and it'll all be digital information. It will sound exactly the same as when I**

played it. And it'll be clear as a bell and it'll be dynamite. Right there in his home as if I were playing it with him. We just transfer the messages to each other digitally. The quality is perfect. Now, a lot of people would argue about that, but to me that's great, that's efficient. Now I don't have to go there and move into a hotel, and raise the $20,000 budget or even hassle with England! I think that's a great thing. In fact, that's *more* communication, not less. I can play on your record if you're anywhere.[25]

For most rock fans there's a deep-rooted sense of difference between "real" musical instruments—guitars, drums, sax, piano, voice—and false ones, electronic devices of all sorts. The rationale is straightforward: musicians can be seen to *work* on real instruments, there is a direct relationship between physical effort and sound. But from musicians' point of view it makes no sense. For a producer-musician like Nile Rogers, quoted above, "music" is whatever sounds a musician shapes, using whatever devices necessary to produce and organize them. In his words, "technology just allows composers to be more creative than they have been. I mean, I can't play the French horn, but I have some great French horn sounds in my Synclavier. It allows me to interpret the French horn the way *I* hear it."

In celebrating technology for increasing his control of sounds (and doing away with the social relations of production) Rogers is, though, being as misty-eyed about the meaning of "music" as the rock fans who equate expression and sweat. Music isn't just what musicians do, but what they think they can do, what they're technically able to do. As another musician, Chris Cutler, has pointed out, the increasing use of sampling devices and preprogramed synthesizers means that as producers musicians are, in fact consumers, working with commercial sounds that have been made *for* them.[26] In general, what we hear as music, whether as musicians or as listeners, whether in enjoying it or pushing against its limits, is produced by social forces that have little to do with either individual genius or eternal harmonies. Technology is the most obvious social factor. The electronic microphone allowed us to hear aspects of performance that we'd never heard before, amplifying intimacy. Magnetic tape made possible the construction of music that never existed or could exist as a single event. Compact disc players are now giving people a new idea of good sound, one without distraction, in which the ear is drawn to the surface of the track, the moment of musical production, with no reference to its context or surrounding noise. CD, as the "truest" sound, is thus the most false; we interpret as an act of human music making a play of electronic pulses.

The point of these examples, though, is not just that music is "unnatural"—the measure of sound quality keeps changing, what we listen out for is a matter of convention—but also that such conventions have to be understood in terms of the economic forces encouraging us to own certain listening equipment, to buy certain musical instruments. Recording "fidelity," as a marketing term, depends on an ideology of what listening should be. In pop the most dramatic effect of techno-economic forces was probably the time limit placed on song by the original phonograph discs, which determined Tin Pan Alley formulas and even defined the meaning of jazz improvisation. In general, to realize its earning potential as a commodity, music has to be organized as something in which owners *can* claim rights. To put this another way, the peculiar capitalist argument that music is a *thing* can only be maintained by an elaborate legal structure.

The present music copyright system is derived from nineteenth century literary law: what was protected was the musical *script*; the law was designed to protect sheet music publishers from piracy. The original musical commodity was thus a score, and even as the law changed to take account of audio recording—a new way of fixing sounds—the song, defined as a particular combination of harmony, melody, and

lyric, remained the object of legal protection. The most important collecting agencies for copyright fees are still the publishing societies (ASCAP and BMI in the U.S.A., PRS in Britain).
Registering a song with them involves putting it in written
form, but what's most significant about this is what is not
copyrightable—timbre, rhythm, the very qualities that became, with the rise of recording, central to pop pleasure. (And
that has served as one way in which black musicians have
been exploited by the pop industry, via the law's definition of
music in European rather than Afro-American terms).

The myth of rock depended on copyright law, on the organization of production around "artists" and "works"; these
terms remained serviceable, even as rock appeal became
more dependent on collective studio techniques rather than
individual writing or performing skills. The new threat to
copyright reflects a different issue: not who "wrote" a record
but at what digital moment it was finished.

This question arises most obviously from the development
of computer sampling instruments like the Fairlight, which
enables players to quote an aspect of someone else's music—
their sound—which was previously unprotected because technically uncopyable. A musician who quoted, say, the melody
line from a Beatles' song expected to be charged for its use;
the legal battle was how much of a phrase constituted a
quote. Now he or she can directly quote McCartney's bass,
and the legal implications of this are confused—particularly
as in practice, sampling has so far been mostly a rhythmic
matter. Beat patterns have been filched from every possible
source, partly because their contribution to the success of a
song is not easily recognized (the average listener—or judge
—finds it much easier to spot a secondhand tune) and partly
because over the years rock and funk musicians have been
most imaginative in their use of drum, bass, and rhythm
guitar. And, anyway, the technology makes samplers most
useful for their repetitive effects.

Sampling challenges the legal definition of music in three

respects. First, it undermines musicians' control of their own sounds, and initial court cases in Britain and the U.S.A. suggest that it is easier to prove ownership of one's voice (like James Brown) than one's drum or bass noise.

Second, sampling raises new questions about "public domain." If a track is sampled from the streets, does its original publisher have any rights in it? Can Abba or Led Zeppelin still claim to own a harmony or riff once it's part of the urban soundscape? Can Ronald Reagan? His speeches turned up, cut and mixed, on a plethora of dance tracks, and as far as I know he has never asked for a return. Culturcide recorded a diatribe over a "real" Springsteen track. Is this the same gesture as sticking a moustache on a reproduction Mona Lisa?

Anglo-American copyright law is not a statement of ethical principle but a device to sustain a *market* in ideas, and until now, courts have treated copyright issues in financial terms, allowing as "fair" uses of a sound or image that do not interfere with rights holders' chances to make money for themselves. The third sampling issue concerns "fair use," the strand of the law that protects the public's interest, and prevents cultural rights owners from restricting use of their material unduly. When digital recording is the norm, the "listener" will have as much opportunity to unfix and refix a piece of music at home as the "producer" in the studio. Recordings in this scenario will simply be sounds packaged for convenience in one combination but available to everyone for deconstruction. The music consumer of the future will thus be "active" in new ways—editing out the bass, feeding in a drum line from another package altogether, adding their own voice. This will certainly challenge the distinction between creator and consumer that copyright law currently takes for granted. Sound suppliers should clearly be paid for their efforts, but whether artistic copyright will be the best way of treating such labor is an open question.

The issue has arisen where production/consumption already meet on the dance floor, for example, where disc jockeys have long used records as source material for their own works, and in the marketing campaigns for digital instruments. The other side of the consumer-as-producer is, after all, the producer-as-consumer, and musicians are already being sold sound packages, guaranteed "copyright clear." Bill Drummond of the Justified Ancients of Mu Mu, a British "sampling band," responded to Abba's threat to sue him for using a sample of "Dancing Queen" by threatening to sue the computer company that provided him with the sample in the first place.

Sampling, in short, calls into question the principles that underpin copyright law: first, that a musical work has an author, a creator whose rights must be protected, and, second, that there is a clear distinction between an "original" work and its "copy." From the record company's point of view this means an increasing number of legal disputes about who owns what. The rise of the rock star as a corporate trademark, for instance, means that image is as important a source of income as sound, and image makers—the packagers and designers—may thus lay claim to a copyright on the stars themselves (just as studio producers and engineers now expect a royalty). From a fan's point of view, what is going on here is the systematic dismantling of the belief system that sustained rock 'n' roll, the idea that a recognizable person (or group of persons) made a specific noise. Even as attention shifted from stage to studio technique, we still always heard of tracks as *authored*.

This way of listening is breaking down now in a number of respects. For a start, as Robert Christgau has argued,[27] the visual context of music making has changed. Rock 'n' roll is now a normal feature of television and film entertainment, on routine display in department store and bar videos, and a presence on advertising billboards. For an increasing number of rock fans the meaning of "live" performance, the look of music "in reality" therefore comes from its ubiquitous simulation. This is an example of what we might call the Baudrillard effect: a concert feels real only to the extent that it matches its TV reproduction; even Bruce Springsteen's shows are now experienced in terms of their video imagery.

No wonder the idea of authorship is getting harder to hang on to. Not only have all distinctions between authenticity and artifice (musician and engineer) broken down, but there is no longer even an obvious moment when someone says *this* is the work that we have (re)produced. All pop records are issued now, it seems, in various versions, and such market choice (do you want the club mix? the radio mix? the rock mix? the teen mix?) effectively discredits the claim that any of the tracks is *the* work of art. When X remixes Y, who is the "author" of the record? The "basic" track is more obviously a design blueprint than a means of unique expression; the credited performer more like a fashion model than a Van Gogh.

The technological threat to rock's core values—sweat, spontaneity, collective inspiration—has been resisted, of course. Rock bands that depend on tapes to enhance their live sound (as most do) still conceal their use; engineers and disc jockeys are still regarded as "only" craftsmen; stardom still means fronting a track. But our appreciation of music is changing anyway. Most listeners, for example, no longer care that they have no idea what instrument (if any) makes their favorite sound. And the most significant rearguard action against technological change is, as usual, being fought by the music business itself. Software manufacturers are always having to defend ways of making money that derive from the use of obsolete hardware. Records are thus protected as if they were sheet music; digitally produced sounds are being protected as if they were records. This is the perpetual music industry bind: technology undermines profit-taking routines; the state and the law have to be invoked to protect the musical commodity *from* market forces.

# WHO BUYS?

Thorn EMI will attempt to banish the dowdy image of the
TV and audio rental business by offering Yuppies with an
ear and an eye for fashion the chance to rent the best
and most sophisticated in fashion furniture with built-in
hi-fi. . . . Customers will be offered the chance to rent
videos, TVs, compact disc recorders, and even security
systems, all built into or around the most modern
furniture. The scheme is aimed at the sort of well-off
customer who is "highly committed" to sound, vision, and
fashion furniture, and who has an "I want it now"
attitude to the latest. . . . Thorn is already working with
furniture designers on the scheme, and compact disc
players linked to speakers in designer tables and videos
that allow you to check at the same time if the kiddies
are sleeping tight are among the "bundled" packages
promised.[28]

The youth share of leisure and consumer expenditure
began to decline in the 1970s simply as a matter of demographics. The rising levels of youth unemployment meant too
that teenagers now had relatively less spare cash and remained more financially dependent on their families. In the
end, though, the effect of these material changes was not that
record companies ceased to service youth but, rather, that the
"youth market" began to describe new taste targets; on the
one hand, 25-to-40-year-olds, the baby boomers grown up,
the audience for AOR radio and *Rolling Stone*; on the other
hand, children, early teens, the audience for *Smash Hits* and
MTV. The average age of fans of the biggest eighties pop
stars (like Michael Jackson and Madonna) is certainly lower
than it was ten years ago. (Even an obviously adolescent

group like the Beastie Boys seems more like a child's cartoon version of punk than the real thing.) But what's most striking about the late 1980s music scene is the continuing popularity of rock dinosaurs. When the Grateful Dead, Fleetwood Mac, and Genesis dominate the charts, it's tradition that's being celebrated, not novelty, whatever the actual age of the fans.

In material terms, the traditional rock consumer—the "rebellious" teenager—is no longer the central market figure; the most obvious teen musics, like heavy metal and hard core punk, are thus now marginal to mainstream pop culture (however commercially successful some of their proponents). At the same time, though, the *ideology* of the teen remains crucial for what rock is supposed to mean, and, not surprisingly, the effects of this gap between rock theory and rock practice have been confusing. On the one hand the 1980s marked the rise of yuppie rock, in which the ideology of teen is translated into an affluent adult life-style; on the other hand, there has been a moral panic about the rock "threat" to the family that seems like a throwback to the fifties.

The sudden emergence of organizations like the Parents' Music Resource Center, campaigning for the protection of children from the sounds of sex and drugs (while assuring us, like Tipper Gore, they have nothing against rock 'n' roll) was partly the effect of rock's move out of the teen bedroom into the family living room via two 1980s phenomena: music television and aerobics. But what matters most about the PMRC is not that it exists, but that it has been successful: records are now labeled with reference to "explicit" content, civic auditoriums take more note of who they book, MTV is more concerned to broadcast "wholesomely."

The music industry has gone along with such parental concerns not because it too has swung to the moral right, nor even out of a cynical calculation that if it plays along with the senators' wives in support of moral protection, the senators will acquiesce in the industry's campaign for commercial protection. No, the record industry's thinking is more straightforward: the obstreperous teen market is a minority matter; the bulk of pop profits now come from music's use in mainstream entertainment. As campaigns are fought around youth sexuality and drug use, it is commercially important for the music industry to appear to be on the right side. This is another aspect of the record industry's charity work: rock musicians are now *responsible*.

Meanwhile, yuppies—orderly adults with money to spend and good training in rock consumption—seem to be even better news for the record industry than they were the first time around when they were teens. The result is all those sixties tracks digitally remastered for the compact disc catalog. In the long-term, though, servicing this market may not be as straightforward as it seems. CDs have sold well, back catalogs have indeed been profitable, but the problem is how to break *new* yuppie stars. What every record company wants, now that these catalogs are exhausted, is a new Dire Straits —an act whose adult appeal is not based on nostalgia. The problem is that in breaking new stars, companies still think in terms of teen media. What they have to learn, as a British CBS executive explained to me, is that what matters in yuppie sales is not radio or club play but dinner party time. This exec needed his records (Sade was his success story) to be heard over the quiche on Friday evenings, bought with the groceries on Saturday mornings.

But even this may miss the point. Yuppies aren't like teenagers but older; they constitute a different *sort* of market altogether. They weren't out there waiting to be discovered; they were defined by advertisers in the first place. "We like them," explained advertising man Mark Cranmer, with reference to Q, a new male music magazine from the *Smash Hits* stable, and *Arena*, a new male fashion magazine from *The Face* stable, both designed for 25-to-35-year-olds. "They're a healthy addition for products such as lager, as well as for fashion and records." [29] But records are the least important of these goods. The most profitable musical services the record industry can provide are the sounds—the authentic, familiar, *soulful* sounds—that are used to sell everything else.

# CONCLUSION

**I**n the last ten years or so the organization of popular music production and consumption has changed sufficiently to invalidate most of the assumptions on which rock culture rests. Commercial popular music no longer depends on the sale of *records;* it can no longer be understood in terms of a *fixed sound object;* it is no longer made in terms of a particular sort of audience, *rebellious youth.* In short, the *rock* system of music making no longer determines industry activity.

The crisis this created for record companies in the late 1970s has now been ridden out, though it is not yet clear what will happen in the future: much depends on technological and legal disputes still unresolved. What is clear is that some dearly-held academic rock assumptions can no longer be sustained.

The first assumption is that people have musical "needs" that are ill-met by a conservative industry and therefore periodically bust open the market's constraints. This assumption misunderstands the dynamic of mass cultural change. The major disruptive forces in music in this century have been new devices, technological breakthroughs developed by electronics manufacturers who have very little idea of their potential use. The only lesson to be learned from pop history (besides the fact that industry predictions are always wrong) is that the devices that succeed best in the market are those that increase consumer control of their music. The industry's commercial task has not been to persuade people to do something they otherwise wouldn't (buy a record, rent a video) but to ensure that whatever they do do brings in a financial return.

The second assumption is that rock articulates the concerns of individuals or groups *to whom commercialization then happens*. This assumption is based on a belief that there is a distinction between music as human expression and music as commodity. The real point, however, is that what music means—what we *hear* as authentic—is already determined by the technological and economic conditions of its production; it does not exist in any sort of ideal or innocent state.

The third assumption is that rock is a subcultural expression, with particular rock genres not only appealing to particular taste publics but somehow *representing* them. The explicit suggestion is that subcultural music—punk, for example, in which a sound was articulated through a set of conventions formalized in fanzines and club life—is a model for collective expression. The implication is that a truly popular culture in a mass society depends on radical *consumption*.

These assumptions have been particularly important for our understanding of rock politics: as a matter of market struggle between indies and majors; as a matter of street struggle between rebel youth groups and the mainstream; as a matter of ideological struggle between artistic truth and commercial compromise. The story I've told here may therefore seem to carry a message of despair, a message not tempered by its postmodern reinterpretation as an episode in the politics of art: when every experience is simulated, all we can do is celebrate the end of reason. But my own conclusion is different. The collapse of rock's money-making routines actually means that the politics of mass music are about to enter their most exciting phase. The shadowboxing of consumers—revolt into style, taste wars, pop as youth display—is giving way to the material struggle for a piece of the new musical action.

*S e x ,   r o c k ,*

*a n d   i d e n t i t y*

T
H
E

E
N
E
M
Y

W
I
T
H
I
N

**T**he clip opens with a shot of a file, marked with the legend "Ministry of Culture" and a neoconstructivist logo. A hand turns over the cover and stamps "Approved" onto a paper that says: "The Communards: Music Banning Order." Quick cut to a group of young males and females, dressed down in one fashionable London style, purposefully making their way through a typical postindustrial wasteland. Their destination is a warehouse party where they are vetted at the door and stamped with the logo that we have just seen.

A young man with a polo shirt and very short, shaven hair begins to sing devotionally, picked out in a spotlight, that obscures the natural light coming from high, churchlike windows. The crowd in place, the performance starts: the lone singer is joined by a woman, with whom he trades the vocals, and a full, predominantly female band. The clip breaks into bursts of move ment that match its subject: a fast, synthetic dance number.

As the clip settles down, the customary performance shots —close-ups, long shots from within the audience—are intercut with images that follow on from the opening, which are meant to provide a narrative. A good-looking young man— tousled blond hair, square jaw, blue eyes—is picked out of the crowd by the camera, as an object of desire and as a protagonist. As the song slows into a prolonged instrumental and scat vocal vamp, the "plot" thickens.

The young man runs down a warehouse corridor in an echo of countless paranoid movies; he is at first alone, and then pursued by two leather-jacketed, booted messengers—themselves inept approximations of Cocteau's motorcycled angels of death in *Orphée*. As they catch up with him, there is a very quick cut to an "inquisitor" figure. As the young man is hauled up, and we get a closer look at this figure—shaved head, impenetrable sunglasses, and mustache—not a million miles away from still current gay "clone" signifiers. As the instrumental break winds up to the song's final verse, this inquisitor hands a walkie-talkie to the young man.

We next see the young man back in the crowd; this time he is distinguished from the rest of the celebrants. As the peformance draws to a close, he mutters into the walkie-talkie and turns away. The clip cuts to the messengers, the young man, and the inquisitor on a balcony: as the music ends, a searchlight is turned on and the party breaks up with sounds of panic added onto the soundtrack. After a last, lingering look at the young man, the clip fades on a close-up of the inquisitor—the instrument of a society intent on stamping out desire and difference.

# LOST YOUTH

In 1986, the second best selling 45 in England was the Communards' version of Harold Melvin and the Bluenotes'

"Don't Leave Me This Way." The 1975 original was peak period Sound of Philadelphia—a product of Philadelphia International Records, the label that took over as the dance music factory of America after Motown lost its grip in the early seventies—and an English top ten hit the following year. Anonymous and functional in the original, the song's revival at the hands of a white, synthetic pop group invested the song with a whole set of new meanings—an excellent example of the dialectic between English youth culture and Black American dance music then reaching its apogee.

Since the early eighties, Black American pop—particularly sixties soul and Motown, but also contemporary dance music like hip-hop—has been at the heart of new (or postmodernist) English pop: the unifying strand behind the loose movement that, from Wham! to Duran Duran and the Eurythmics, has been the second successful English attempt at repackaging American music and selling it worldwide. In England, black dance music is mass market music and has been since the sixties. On top of its deep populist roots lies another, subcultural factor: its assumption as a style by a whole generation of musicians and its position as a touchstone for various cultural ideas about "authenticity" and "community."

These are important in England for various reasons. As an African-American form, pop music is not indigenous, being rather an exotic import from America in the mid-fifties. English musicians have had to *learn* styles rather than pluck them out of their immediate environment, and, because of various structural defects in English society, English pop is enmeshed in a vortex of social, cultural, and political demands unfamiliar to most Americans since the late sixties. It comes *loaded.* The idea of "community"—however illusory—has become important as a way to describe the organization of disparate groups of people, united only by the fragile bond of common age, that is still the dream of youth culturists.

This idea has had a renewed relevance in England over the past few years, as an attempt to counter not only the fragmentation of youth culture, but also the increasing atomization of English society. Left ideologists posit the idea of "community" (often tinged with nostalgia for the working-class past) as an alternative to New Right privatization of our economic and social life. During this period, the diminished traces of youth cultural activity have become merged with this New Left ideal—most noticeably in the 1986 launch of Red Wedge, a youth-cult organization affiliated with the Labour Party and supported by several English pop stars.

Black American music is the sound of this movment; it boosts left cultural ideas about "authenticity." Thirty years ago it might have been Woody Guthrie; today, it's Bobby Womack.

The Communards' commitment to this community is further reinforced by the factor that distinguishes them in the pop marketplace; their presence as "out gay" pop stars. They emerged from English gay politics, which has the same organizing force as in America, albeit on a much smaller scale: this makes them committed to "coming out" (declaring their homosexuality unambiguously), to provide role models for gay behavior, and to speaking on behalf of a gay community vulnerable after the onset of AIDS in England in 1983.

This is made explicit in everything that they do, and is implicit in their choice of talismanic references: the orchestrated, protodisco sound of the original "Don't Leave Me This Way" is much more indicative of gay subcultural taste than Stax or deep soul could ever be. And, in a direct link between past and present, they cover the song in a style that takes its lineage from Philly International's lush, synthetic tones: High Energy (or Hi NRG), a kind of speeded-up, camped-up disco.

You might be thinking that all this stuff about authenticity and community is an awful lot to load onto aspirant black musicians, and you'd be right. How do you reconcile the fact that, for instance, the original production of sixties black dance music was, as often as not, highly *inauthentic*? Take Stax or Atlantic: most of the records now revered as "classics" were produced by interracial bands (often comprising middle-class blacks) to be crossover hits. Metaphors are handy but the reality behind them is awkward.

This is where the contradictions start. The Communards' mix of Philly International and High Energy is an authentic subcultural use of inauthentic cultural forms. This is fine as far as the gay and left audiences are concerned: they'll pick up the signals. To the wider pop audience not concerned with these debates, "Don't Leave Me This Way" arrives as a typical postmodern dance record, a product representative of a style that flaunts the inauthenticity that is at pop's core. Like Sinitta's "So Macho"—a gay cult item that also became a big English hit in 1986—the record's meaning becomes ambiguous on exposure to the mass market; it is ripe for takeover by readings that affirm rather than challenge the status quo.

The video of "Don't Leave Me This Way" is full of disjunctions that, as often happens, reveal a subtext beneath the clip's overt message. They are exacerbated by the visual shorthand that is the video director's stock in trade, and by the use of images pilfered from recognizable sources (famous films, earlier ad campaigns) that are familiar to the point of archetype. Reclaiming these archetypes is a tricky business.

Reading the video is further complicated by the way in which it is transmitted. Almost every English TV program plays the video not from the very beginning, but from the point where the musical theme starts and the band comes in. The overt message is clear at this point: a sense of pride and community, and a near inversion of the standard pop video glamor tactic—instead of the customary female model, a good looking man is singled out by the cameras as an object of desire. The clip was usually faded out before the final chorus, leaving—on first viewing at least—the narrative as a confusing, disquieting blur.

The problem for the Communards is that in England, the idea of "community" doesn't have the same romantic force that it has in America. For various reasons—class structure, national archetypes, and even physical space—English notions of community tend to be local and highly specific. English pop reflects this; despite its rhetoric, it has always been more about difference than community. In America, an audience might go: "Look at us! We're the same!" In England, the attitude would be: "Look at me! I'm different!"

The idea of pop as a youth cult community was a product of sixties affluence when it entered the language of television and advertising, media that stress the consumerism at youth culture's heart. The Communards' use of the audience in their clip is not unlike the way the audience is draped around the studio to frame performers in England's principal chart show, "Top of the Pops." There, a visible audience does not suggest community, except in the vaguest terms, but is understood as a basic formal device for the TV presentation of pop. Despite its sensitivity, the Communards' clip fits only too well with the "Top of the Pops" format.

A standard reading of the performance would therefore miss any hint of specific (gay-left) community and instead concentrate on the narrative. In the clip, the "star"—the young man—is first shown as a celebrant, one of "us"; by slow degrees, he is revealed to have betrayed the Communards ("us," the community) to a totalitarian, Big Brother figure, who is himself homosexual. This reading reveals another deeper archetype: the linking of homosexuality with treason and treachery.

Americans will be familiar with this idea from the McCarthy era, when it was thought that homosexuals became spies because both led double lives. (It was, of course, entirely fitting that the Inquisitor, Senator McCarthy, was himself bisexual). In England, this paranoid fantasy became reality, with the May 1951 defection of diplomats Guy Burgess and Donald MacLean and the subsequent thirty-year unraveling of a predominantly homosexual, Soviet spy ring that had penetrated deep into the heart of the establishment. In the dying days of 1979, Anthony Blunt, a knight and the Keeper of the Queen's Pictures, was unmasked as the final link in the chain.

These events still reverberate. Blunt, Burgess, and MacLean are folk devils (or heroes), conjoining several English nightmares: the problem was not that they were extraordinarily deviant, but that they shared and expressed values that enabled them to pass undetected in the upper echelons of English society, in Blunt's case for over forty-five years. Homosexuality is heavily bonded into the English upper and upper-middle classes, but is, of course, sublimated: the spies' real crime was to make what was implicit explicit, to make what was private public. In doing so, they violated a fundamental taboo.

In this way, the power of (homo)sexuality is acknowledged. As Jonathan Dollimore writes: "For a variety of complex reasons society needs its deviants; in some cases for example a dominant culture needs its inferiors, its others, in order to consolidate itself. Often overlapping with such consolidation is a process of displacement: the demonized abnormal other, whose alienness reinforces through contrast the rightness of normality, serves at the same time as a scapegoat for normality's own sexual and not-so-sexual anxieties."[1] All of us are policed and betrayed by our sexuality.

Within this vortex (given new terrors from AIDS), the Communards' deeply ambiguous video stands poised between the conscious and the subconscious. It mixes positive assertion with self-hatred, political idealism with commercial pragmatism; its flaws reveal the relations of race, gender, and youth that have always been an important, if hidden, part of pop music. Pop marks the cultural visibility of the formerly invisible, the assumption of power by the disenfranchised. It represents the present and the future: that above all is why it is hated by those who wish to perpetuate the past.

# CONSUMER TRAINEES

**The young were living mostly in exile, but exile gave them possibilities of which they had seldom dreamed before. Everything around them became slightly abnormal, the new occupation, the environment, the dress they wore, the physical and emotional climate. The concrete things of the past, like postal addresses, timetables, road signs, became less probable and friendships became all-important because it was unlikely that they would last. Nearly all of them, willingly or unwillingly, became creatures of the moment, living in an everlasting present; the past had vanished, the future was uncertain.[2]**

The appearance of the teenager at the end of the Second World War made youth a symbol of the postwar world, a world which had turned on its head, where alienation was the norm. Youth was now the receptor of adult fears, projections, and fantasies; it became the focus of desire, with all its ambiguities. The teenager was not only a harbinger but a "consumer trainee," "important in the market place as an innovator and a style setter for older people."[3] In his/her inchoate form, the consumer dream could be made flesh.

This dream was crucial to the emerging postwar democracy. Both in America and in England, the war had shaken existing power structures and in Europe there was a definite postwar shift toward socialism. The idea that consumption could channel these troubling impulses for capitalism was seized on by opportunistic politicians. In 1959, for instance, Richard Nixon attributed the success of the American (as opposed to the Russian) system to the fact that "44 million families in America own 56 million cars, 50 million television sets, 143 million radio sets, and 31 million of those families own their own homes."[4] In 1957, Conservative Prime Minister Harold MacMillan made one of the most famous statements in postwar English politics when he said, "let's be frank about it: some of our people have never had it so good."[5]

The democracy of consumption, in which everyone was equal before the checkout counter, was double-edged. Although in Marxist terms an opiate, consumerism was, for many years, a quite inefficient agent of social control. The technology that is at the heart of consumer mass production is, in itself, neutral and difficult to control, failing, as it does, to recognize the limits of range and access that many would like to put on it. And, for a long time, the wish to control consumerism was not there: the overwhelming drive on the part of capital to find new markets and new products steamrollered previously rigid moral codes and social boundaries. In this new democratic ideal, previously marginal subcultures were drawn into the net and used as source material. These outcasts had long-developed codes and metaphors to deal with the alienation that was now threatening everyone.

"To some extent, the teenage market—and in fact, the very notion of the teenager—had been created by the businessmen who exploit it,"[6] claimed a long New Yorker profile of Eugene Gilbert in 1958. In fact, Gilbert, who opened his market research company—Gil-Bert Teen Age Services—in 1945, merely codified existing youth trends and made projections from the available demographics.[7] Although youth was not highly visible in the thirties—or, at least, not in the period's principal sociological document, Robert Lynd's 1937 Middletown in Transition—it had already been established in the 1920s as a category and a special interest group. A postwar baby boom—the birthrate jumped from 2.9 million to 3.8 million in America between 1945 and 1947—stimulated the juices and helped to pump in the money that turned the idea of youth into mass market reality. Teenagers had a new economic and symbolic power and from it, cultural and political power eventually followed.

This was a gradual process but already well-established

by 1958. If "the typical preteenage-era adolescent . . . was part of the family, formed by adult values even when he was challenging the grown-ups who held them," then the postwar youth was newly assertive, had an acute sense of *difference* from the adult world. A break had been made. The new emotional map was explored in J. D. Salinger's famous novel of 1950, *The Catcher in the Rye*,[8] in which Holden Caulfield quits prep school for an existential, solo flight into New York's nightlife. What was new was both the assumption that this was a possible course of action—even a desirable one—and the book's obsession with sex and sexual difference. Caulfield's New York dream is filled with people more exotic than his most lurid fantasies: "flits," "working girls," "perverts and morons," "gray-haired, distinguished-looking guys" who put on women's clothes. Caulfield recounts this in breathless prose, as light begins to penetrate the deepest shadows.

# TEEN DREAMS

I'd been singing "Tutti Frutti" for years, but it never struck me as a song you'd *record*. I didn't go to New Orleans to record no "Tutti Frutti." Sure, it used to crack the crowds up when I sang it in the clubs, with those risqué lyrics: "Tutti Frutti, good booty/If it don't fit, don't force it/You can grease it, make it easy. . . ."[9]

Little Richard's song neatly illustrates the social and cultural changes that were occurring in the early fifties despite (or in counterpoint to) a climate of fear and illiberalism. While not a huge "pop" hit—the song was diluted by a very white and very successful Pat Boone cover version—"Tutti Frutti" had a massive, worldwide impact. It's a classic example of a cross-over code: Little Richard was from the South, homosexual, and black—triply disadvantaged by prewar standards—and his song was coded for an audience of social misfits. Censoring themselves for the pop market, Richard and his producer cut lyrics to the point of nonsense, yet the song retained its implications: young whites celebrated its very lack of overt meaning—which made absolute sense, not only as a cover for what was behind it, but as a surefire way to exclude adults.

R&B was different from the pre-war black music of the blues, although no less coded: urban, heavily amplified, and much more assertive.[10] It began to cross over to whites from the early fifties: in 1951 Alan Freed was the first radio DJ to capture teenagers for R&B, renamed "rock 'n' roll," for the new market; in 1952 he promoted one of the first interracial concerts. Because of the racial structure of a conservative music industry, it took until 1956, though, for the music to break into the mass pop market in an undiluted (but still white) form, with the extraordinary success of Elvis Presley.[11]

The furor that greeted Presley's appearance was an index of very deep white American fears about blacks and sexuality —the two were customarily interlinked. Presley's genius was to unite two "outcast" but populist musical forms—white trash country with Deep South R&B—and, almost subconsciously, to embody his difference with a series of electric, erotic movements. The music industry was in a quandary: the stuff was disgusting but it *sold.* The major companies pursued a successful policy of burying popular black songs under tepid white covers and, when public demand made concealment impossible, the Dionysiac presence of stars like Little Richard was presented—in films like *Don't Knock the Rock* and *The Girl Can't Help It*—as an anthropological exercise to a politely bemused, all-white audience. It had to be *interpreted.*

Just like youth sexuality (of which it was the first confident expression), rock 'n' roll was potentially explosive; just as worrying was the extent to which it was the iceberg-tip of a vast, hitherto disenfranchised mass underneath. The adult response to this threat, both conscious and subconscious, veered between exploitation and condemnation. Most effective was a kind of policing, whereby the potential for disturbance contained in these dangerous teen years could be *trained,* guided into "planning a career or a home, looking toward mature human relationships." Nowhere is this more obvious than in the new media that sprang up for young women: not only because young women are frequently the locus for adult sexual fears and fantasies, but also because young women were in the commercial teenage vanguard—a fact still barely recognized in most accounts of pop culture. As the *New Yorker* stated in 1958, "the female half of the teenage market has been studied more extensively than the male."[12] *Seventeen*— whose creed was to cover everything that "concerns, excites, annoys, pleases, and perplexes the girl between thirteen and nineteen"—was first published in 1944, predating (and in fact stimulating) Gilbert's codification of the youth market.

Magazines like *Seventeen* and its competitors exhibited the riches of this female market in the advertisements they carried for clothes, for self-improvement, but most of all, for beauty products and cosmetics—on which, according to a 1958 Gilbert survey, young women spent twenty-six cents out of every dollar. The sexual threat of "petticoat power" is implied by the elaboration used in its control: A 1950 *Teen Age Book* resolves serious questions like "How Old Is Old Enough for Make-Up,"[13] while Abigail Van Buren's 1959 *Dear Teenager*[14] contains a labyrinthine set of codes designed to placate peer anxieties, under chapter headings like "The Dating Game" (twelve subdivisions), "Bluejean Biology" (five), and "Here's Looking at You" (ten).

The adult worries coded into such manuals had a sound basis in fact; young women dictated the new sexual map. Their hysteria, triggered by key pop figures and film stars, was one of the first indices of the new age, the factor that made postwar stardom and sexuality different from what had gone before. Only the extraordinary scenes that had occurred on the death in 1926 of Rudolf Valentino—the man who, in linking sex with androgyny and death, had set the high wa-

termark of interwar fandom—had hinted at what was soon
to become commonplace: the dervish power of aroused young
women.

It would be incorrect to seek standard feminist meanings in
this assertiveness and the purchasing power that it marked,
however. *Seventeen* reacted to demographic trends—in 1958,
for instance, 50 percent of all women marrying for the first
time were under twenty—and soon service magazines like
*Ladies' Home Journal* came into being. The primacy of young
women in the early teenage era was soon challenged by a
male revolt. the massive success of rock 'n' roll organized
young men into consumption, both as producers and consumers. Rock shifted the focus of the teenage industries away from
beauty products into music—where it remains.

Pop music was now defined as a male preserve: both in
the primacy of male stars (how many *well-known* female rock
'n' rollers are there?) and in the way it was consumed, in its
*appreciation*. The typical attitude is captured in a 1956 music
paper headline: "Are Bobbysoxers Musically Ignorant?"[15] The
excitement of young women was devalued in favor of male
preoccupations like "technique," "artistry," and "authenticity"
—a division which still persists today. Yet even as "passive
consumers"—for this is how young female fans were patron-
izingly seen by the dominant culture—the female market
was the backbone of the music industry: if debarred from
participation in production, it would express its power in other
ways. Of these, the most important was in the representation
of male sexuality.

The crucial male figure at this point was not Presley or
Brando but James Dean.[16] Dean's continuing power as an
archetype—16-year-olds still pin his picture on their walls,
thirty years after his death—lies not just in necrophilia but in
the fact that he embodies, for all time, the neurotic transience
and possibility of the teenager. In Dean, everything is in flux.
His identity in his most emblematic film, "Rebel Without a
Cause," is so fragmented that he appears as more than an

outsider, as a sleepwalker vainly trying to learn the language of an alien dreamscape. As importantly, his sexuality is highly androgynous, not only through the bizarre love triangle he shares with Natalie Wood and Sal Mineo, but also in his uncanny enactment of the "passivity of the adored object"[17] that was the new condition of stardom. Masculinity was now being defined by the female gaze. Dean crystallized male identity in perpetual motion, a most disturbing occurrence when "sexual alienation, one of capitalism's foundations, implies that the social body is polarized in a masculinity"[18] of which "stability" is one of the most vital self-conceptions.

This is to apply hindsight; at the time, all these factors just meant one thing to adult Americans: our kids are turning into (the) Martians (that we can't admit to being). Their projections of fear and disturbance were correspondingly powerful. Just as a sequence of science fiction movies turned Cold War worries into metaphor, so the rash of "juvenile delinquent" movies from the mid-fifties on dramatized adult fears about youth sexuality and purchasing power, and the kind of future that it represented. By 1958, this had got to the stage that, according to the *New Yorker*, "the first association that most adults have with the word 'teenager' is 'juvenile delinquent'."[19] In the then highly controversial *Blackboard Jungle*, Glenn Ford plays the teacher who, faced with a classroom of teens exhibiting an electric hostility, divides and conquers. The bad seeds are isolated and the rest, well, they're just folks like everyone else. Despite the radical packaging—Bill Haley's "Rock Around the Clock" played over the credits—*Blackboard Jungle* was designed to allay adult fears.

These projections were carried one step further in 1957's *I Was a Teenage Werewolf*, where the bad seed was metamorphosed into a folk devil. As Peter Biskind suggests, "the werewolf turned on by a nubile bobbysoxer is a monster from the id. Born to be bad, Tony cannot be cured, only killed."[20] But despite the attempts of these and other films to, at best, socialize problem teens or, at worst, express a psychotic level of hostility, they were unsuccessful in resolving the problems they addressed. Contemporary teenagers reveled in their depiction as aliens, took what they wanted from the flims, and rejected the rest. "Rock Around the Clock," for example, was a massive hit as a result of its exposure and, in England at least, became the signal for exactly the kind of youth rioting "condemned" by *Blackboard Jungle*.

## LIVING DOLLS

To Europeans the American GIs who started to flood the continent after 1942 appeared not so much as aliens— that was indisputable—but as Gods, messengers of the new cargo cult of consumerism. The attraction of the American brand name had been established, in England at least, by the century's teens: here was the first chance to consummate this love affair, to see this mythic world "live." To Europeans in the third year of war the sheer physical impact of the GIs was enormous: their very energy and health symbolized the possibilties of the postwar future.

This new world would be one in which America had a considerable stake. The war had not only boosted America's powerhouse economy, but had overturned its isolationist position of the twenties and thirties. The fact that America, not England or any other of its allies, was the real winner of the war, made it look outwards: this was the start of an economic hegemony that still pertains today. This economic takeover was presaged culturally: the GIs, for instance, not only offered hope but nylons, chocolates, cigarettes, and new dance music as well. The desire that they epitomized went straight to the heart much more effectively than any political manifesto could have done: by 1944, George Orwell noted that "There are great numbers of English people who are partly Americanised in language and, one ought to add, in moral outlook."[21]

Forty years on, the American consumer dream appears less benign, but at the time it offered a seductive view of the future that was shared by millions. Its attraction—as in the United States in the twenties—was the idea that *anybody could join in*. And because this process was delayed materially in England, much in the same way it had been in the United States, the appeal of the idea was intensified. The end of the war coincided with the American cancellation of the land-lease agreement and Britain was virtually bankrupt: the new government was forced to promote rationing of most basic products as a social necessity. The tension thrown up by images of future plenty clashing with a continuation of wartime conditions—meat, for instance, was rationed until 1954—was terrific. America's position became ambiguous: on the one hand a beacon to the future, on the other a symbol for strong desires that had to be repressed. Postwar England was swamped by fears about American domination, and a series of moral panics focused on those social groups that embodied change: youth in general and the spiv in particular.[22]

Postwar tensions in England found their expression first in the shadowy figure of the spiv—the black marketeer—who became first a national obsession and then a national archetype. The spiv sold all those products, like nylons, eggs, or chocolates, which were rationed: he became the unofficial agent of desire, disapproved of by the authorities but regarded with an amused tolerance by the population at large. His costume advertised his profession—the lurid tie and exaggerated outline of the American zoot suit, then enjoying a vogue in England—and he commanded a greater sense of space than was usually permitted in a country "where everybody knew their place." Spivs located the early roots of English youth culture, not in generational consumer zones, but in the criminal, territorial areas previously occupied by older working class demons like "artful dodgers" and "hooligans."[23]

As throughout the world, youth became a focus of interest in England during the late forties—and thus a problem. Projecting their own fears, adults thought that young people's restlessness and delinquency, their alienness, reflected their dreams of America and new worlds. A 1948 poll revealed that 58 percent of those under thirty would emigrate if they could. In the early fifties, those worries found a new figure: the cosh boy,[24] a younger spiv, was synonymous with a new kind of random, vicious—one might almost say American—violence. Yet he was quickly succeeded on the streets—and soon, in the public mind—by a figure who, in a blaze of peacock finery, connected old class fears with the new, classless definition of youth as a discrete category—the Edwardian, or teddy boy.

What marked the Edwardian out from all previous "groups" was his clothing: he was a walking signifier of the rebellion against strict English class codes. The year 1951 had seen the reelection of a Conservative government, under wartime patriarch Winston Churchill. The result was a climate in which "the same mood of an old upper and upper-middle-class order safely restored dominated almost every area of national life."[25] The male ideal of the time conformed with "the hegemony of the tweed jacket or the ideology of gentrification";[26] film stars like Michael Dennison or Kenneth More were sexless, decent, full of common sense. The Edwardian's power to shock lay in his transgression of both class and sexual codes.

The term "Edwardian" comes from an upper-class clothing style that was originated in 1947 by England's clothing establishment; it harked back to the pre-First World War "Edwardian era," a time before socialism and formica.[27] It combined detail—velvet collar, fancy waistcoats, slim ties—with shape, waisted and thin, in a reaction to American styles. It was not a great success, but was taken up by homosexuals. In the first two years of the fifties, some of its details were borrowed as insignia by the young criminals who gathered around inner London suburbs like Tottenham or the Elephant and Castle. The first Edwardians, around 1952, grafted the velvet collar and the waistcoat onto an exaggerated shape that, if not quite the zoot suit, was definitely American and highly visible.

This sartorial assertion was new, at least for working-class males. Previously, "dressiness was confined largely to homosexuals. Since they were cut off from the mainstream anyway, both sexually and socially, they had nothing to lose by outrageousness in their clothes."[28] In this way, the Edwardians threw society's disapproval back in its face in a new paradigm: the result was disapproval reinforced by stereotyping and moral panic. Both homosexuals and Edwardians occupied a similar psychic space—"creatures of the moment, living in an everlasting present"[29]—and attracted a similar hatred. Just as gays were stigmatized in the furor that accompanied Burgess and Maclean's defection in 1951, the Edwardians were turned into folk devils by a series of sensational stories of which the notorious Clapham Common murder in summer 1953 was only the first. Such was the penalty of divergence.

Contemporary sociologists detected perversion in the Edwardians' dandyism and obsession with self, but these were the very qualities about to be celebrated in the teenager:[30] the market that could cater to such obsessions was on the point of being established. The influx of rock 'n' roll that began in England from the end of 1954—with Bill Haley's "Shake, Rattle and Roll"—alerted industry and market researchers to youth's commercial potential. Within two years, Edwardians and rock 'n' roll were linked in a peculiarly English synthesis: the first youth life-style package, combining clothes, music, fashion, sex, and space. Homosexuals would have to wait another twenty years before becoming, to whatever degree, rehabilitated through similar conspicuous consumption.[31]

The economic boom that America had enjoyed since the early forties only hit England in the mid-fifties. It was signaled by the extraordinary success of American rock 'n' roll, a massive increase in buying on credit, and the introduction, in September 1955, of commercial television on the American model. By the end of the fifties, England had the second highest expenditure on advertising in the world. Again, the spearhead was youth, the demographics following a postwar baby boom similar to that which had occurred in the United States. Although Eugene Gilbert had visited England in 1956 and pronounced the country not yet ready for youth marketing, the next year another market analyst, Mark Abrams, began researching the document that would become an industry bible, *The Teenage Consumer.*

Abrams took the American line—"The teenager is newly enfranchised, in an economic sense"—but widened the age definition to include those between 15 and 24. *The Teenage Consumer* was part document, part wish fulfillment, opening up vistas of an affluent working-class market and, by extension, a new classless youth society united in consumption. Its figures are interesting: teenagers spent most of their money on clothing, cigarettes, and meals out, in that order, but their significance became clear when teenage expenditure was taken as a percentage of all consumer spending. Key items were cosmetics (24 percent of total spending), cinema (26 percent), bicycles and motorcycles (38 percent)—England was *not* a cruising culture—and records and record players (44 percent).[32] Again, as in America, music was the key to the youth market and came to be the product that denoted youth in the wider marketplace. Between 1953 and 1956, U.K. record production more than doubled.

The question was: What to market? The obvious answer was the new American rock 'n' roll, but this caused problems. The first was familiar: as in America, rock 'n' roll was announced in England by a series of moral panics. After *The Blackboard Jungle* had played to riots in September 1955, everyone wanted in on the act. One incident perfectly illustrates the dynamic of simultaneous exploitation and condemnation. The Bill Haley film *Rock Around the Clock* opened in 1956 to even more riots: in Manchester, a hundred teenagers milled around in the street after the show. This use of public space was translated by the national press the next day into a thousand rioters. England being a small country with a powerful, centralized media, this had immediate repercussions. Teenagers around the country took up the challenge in a series of full-blown riots, the first in a series of ritual dances between media and youth.

The other problem was cultural. In fifties England, the availability of rock 'n' roll was haphazard, reliant on scattershot deals between the two English majors, EMI and Decca, and American companies. There was no doo-wop, not much blackness in general—only Frankie Lymon and Little Richard had major successes—and little of the variety of rockabilly. Despite Haley's early popularity, the brand leader of rock 'n' roll was Elvis Presley, for it was he who united the crucial vectors of youth, pop, and sex. His sexuality was an integral ingredient in pop's power to hook desire into consumption, and, by implication, into the deeper consumer society of which it was the spearhead. But it was alien to England: although Elvis confirmed the American body as the locus of desire, rock 'n' roll itself was seen as another exotic import, like chewing gum or cowboy films. If sexuality was the key selling point of the product—like the tail fin on a new Ford— then it could be isolated and marketed accordingly (and as music, rock 'n' roll was simply heard as a gimmick).

This meant English copies of American rock 'n' roll stars, particularly Elvis, by a music industry that was not mainstream as in the United States, but on the fringes of the main entertainment nexus, variety and show business. Through milieu, London lowlife, and erotic fascination, the English music industry was riddled with a homosexual sensibililty. Imitations of Presley's sexual leer and sallow pout were thus projected in a diluted camp version onto working-class boys rendered passive for mass consumption. A good example was Cliff Richard, who moved quickly from being the best home-grown rocker into an industry plaything: in the words of one of his biggest hits, turned into a "Living Doll." He remains the most archetypal English pop star ever, fittingly without much success in America.

This process was brilliantly captured in Colin MacInnes's *Absolute Beginners*.

> **"I heard one of your arias on the steam, last evening,"
> I told him, "'Separate Separates,' if I remember. Very
> nice."**
> **"Which of the boy slaves was it sung it? Strides
> Vandal? Limply Leslie? Rape Hunger?"**
> **"No, no. . . . Soft-Sox Granite I think it was. . . ."**
> **"Oh, that one. A Dagenham kiddy. He's very new."** [33]

MacInnes, a homosexual outsider, was the only English writer to understand British rock 'n' roll in the fifties, when young males were given lurid, exotic names to approximate American glamor. One "stable" of pop stars had protopop pseudonyms that predate the Andy Warhol superstars by a decade: Duffy Power, Vince Eager, Marty Wilde, Billy Fury, Georgie *Fame*. Wham's manager lays what really happened on the line: "It was surprising that an industry generating so many millions of pounds was prepared to use little more than the manager's sexual tastes as its yardstick of talent. Most of the managers were men, and most of them liked boys." [34]

This equation has haunted English pop and had a profound impact on the masculine image. As Richard Dyer writes: "Im-ages of men must disavow [an] element of passivity caused by putting the body on display if they are to be kept in line with dominant ideas of masculinity-as-activity." [35] Because of the pop process, early English rockers took on the passivity of the adored object even more dramatically than their Ameri-can models. The English genius was not for the music itself, but for its packaging: unable to feel rock 'n' roll as a process or a culture, the English music industry and its performers concentrated on style. They developed a sophisticated concern with image that, together with an obsession with clothes, has dominated English pop ever since.

# THE KINGDOM OF YOUTH

**The adults have commited suicide with Easyway pills, and the teenagers have taken over. Free to smash, loot, and love as they like, the gangs roar through the streets on their expendable brand new motorcycles in search of disappearing stocks of lipstick, petrol, and food. Free of adult control, the youngsters commit every sin but hypocrisy . . . until they meet the future.[36]**

By the mid-sixties, the teenager had gone mainstream: what he or she was, everyone wanted to be. As the postwar baby boomers hit their own teenage years (a child born in 1947 was eighteen in 1965), the religio-economic cycle that had begun in America around the turn of the century reached fruition. The teenager's place in the vanguard of the new consumer revolution conferred upon young people a mythic, quasi-divine status. No longer working-class juvenile delinquents to be patronized or reviled, teenagers became positive role models, harbingers of the new age; middle-class adults, politicians, and institutions began to engage in the "everlasting present"[37] of the teenager's hallmark schizo-world of desire. This shift was announced to the world through a new pop phenomenon.

In England, the Beatles' autumn 1963 breakthrough into hysteria completed a long process of democratization. In the "cool line and witty insolence of youth,"[38] the Beatles embodied the social and cultural changes that had been gestating during the previous ten years. The American dream had hit both the populist and the avant-garde in Britain: the working-class endorsement of teenage and consumer culture was matched by the move towards Pop Art, begun in 1952 by the Independent Group at the ICA. Artists like Richard Hamilton and Eduardo Paolozzi aimed to overthrow "the traditional hierarchical ranking of art and design, a ranking established during the Renaissance." As Dick Hebdige writes, "Pop Art and Pop Art critics were drenched in the rhetoric of the most despised forms of popular culture,"[39] which it was their purpose to regenerate. This was a cultural change that the Beatles, as Liverpool art students, were well able to understand and to exploit: their working-classness was carefully constructed, and cloaked the aristocratic arrogance of die-hard bohemians.[40]

The general intellectual tenor was not elitist but populist. The "satire boom" of the early sixties—a series of revues and television programs that carried cynicism about and attacks on the establishment to a new peak of vitriol—represented an upper-middle class revolt against the static quality of English life, where the "public" and the "private" were irrevocably separated. In June 1963, a scandal broke that appeared to confirm this cynicism and the terminal obsolescence of the old, patriarchal conservative order: the "Profumo Affair"—which involved "call girls," black men (a new folk devil in England), a cabinet minister, and lots of lovingly reported kinky sex—resulted in the resignation of Prime Minister Harold Macmillan (the man who'd announced the consumer boom to English ears) and substantially contributed to the election of a Labour Government the following year. The new "classless" age, which had been presaged by a series of "kitchen sink" films like *Saturday Night and Sunday Morning*—about the northern working class on the move—needed its symbols: the Beatles, in their very class mobility—*Room at the Top* comes to life—were perfect. Their already considerable success was hyped into instant myth.

This was "the return of the repressed." Pop music had been the underdog in England for years; by 1962, it was groping towards a faltering respectability with figures like Adam Faith, a Bobby Darin type who could actually string two words together. The Beatles swapped around the alphabet: Youth now dictated the terms, and it did so in a language that challenged sexual and social barriers. The music with which the Beatles achieved success was an aggressive English translation—filtered through artistic and class politics—of a wide range of American black music. Included as covers on their first two LPs were songs recorded by the Isley Brothers, Smokey Robinson and the Miracles, the Shirelles, and the Marvelettes. This direct black influence, well-credited by the Beatles themselves,[41] was new; it was allied to a firsthand, delinquent experience of hardcore American rockers, many of whom, like Little Richard, Gene Vincent, and Eddie Cochran, remained popular in England long after their U.S. success had faded.

The Beatles' trump card was their packaging, which took the concealed sexual divergence of the previous pop sensibility and made it explicit. Coming out of the established English showbiz style—homosexual manager, "variety" orientation, romantic lyrics—the Beatles became explicitly linked with femininity through their crucial visual hook: long hair. Their fresh masculinity was, meanwhile, reflected in their material and their overall image, which broke the rock 'n' roll pattern, being "neither boys-together aggression nor boy-next-door pathos."[42] This androgynous trend—a deliberate blurring of male/female qualities—was given further impetus by a new English subculture that the Beatles simultaneously heralded and exploited: Mod. Together with the many groups, like the Rolling Stones and the Kinks, that were formed in the wake of the Beatles' success, the mods formed a life-style package that made "swinging" London (copyright *Time* magazine, 1966) the focus of the new world youth style.

The roots of mod are ill-documented: Nik Cohn locates them

in inner suburban stylists,[43] but it's equally likely that they evolved out of the "Italian look" that swept away the cobwebs of the teddy-boy style in 1958. These new dandies had the same sartorial impulses as the early Edwardians, but they were white rather than blue collar; their social organization was not around territory but the new, metropolitan spaces opened up by youth culture. Early mods were called West End boys: gangs of youths who hung around Soho and took in all that the city had to offer. This included sex, drugs, the music (bluebeat or Tamla/Motown)—which was the visible sign of the black immigrant and GI presence—and a clothing style that originated in a Soho street. Richard Barnes, in his textbook on mods, describes it well:

**The only other person we saw was a tall, well-dressed negro who bought a pair of the colored denim hipster trousers. The negro was obviously homosexual, and I realised that homosexuals had been buying that stuff for years. They were the only people with the nerve to wear it, but in the early sixties the climate of opinion was changing, and the Mods were wearing the more effeminate and colourful clothes of Carnaby Street.[44]**

The key to the mods was not homosexuality, though, but an extreme narcissism: they carried the English obsession with clothes and cut to the limit. Barnes again: "Mods were more interested in themselves and each other than in girls. . . . There was a time when Mod boys used makeup and mascara."[45] From 1964 on, the style became so popular that it triggered fresh adult fears about teen takeover. Mod was quickly defined and associated with the objects of two major moral panics. The first, the "mods and rockers" battles at English seaside towns, involved huge gang rumbles. "It was like we were taking over the country,"[46] said one 18-year-old. The other—the amphetamine pills called "purple hearts"—brought to the surface the use of drugs that had always in-

formed "deviant" subcultures (criminals, musicians, bohemian outsiders, and—as viewed by white culture—blacks)
and was now going mass. Drugs (amphetamines and, soon,
marijuana) became attractive to youth both pragmatically—
for pleasure and stimulation—and physically: obliterating
time, drugs locked the consumer into that eternal present that
was the hallmark of the teenage experience. Speed gave
mods the alien, psychotic glare of "quiet, sinister depersonal-
ization" that characterized the child mutants (plotting to take
over the world) of the paranoid 1964 thriller, *Children of the
Damned*. A self-conscious musical translation was the Who's
authentic (but now clichéd) "My Generation,"[47] whose refrain, "Hope I die before I get old"—was delivered in the
perfect confidence of the instant.

The package that hit America on February 7, 1964—announced, fittingly, by the wails of thousands of young women
—contained much of this coded within it. At the time, however, the Beatles were a heavily-hyped novelty, a diversion;
as far as the music industry was concerned, they were a godsend, representing a white male revolt against the assertiveness of the girl groups (which they soon made obsolete) and
the rising flood of black music (which they didn't).[48] Just as
England had packaged the external signifiers of American
rock 'n' roll stars in the fifties, the Beatles' salespoint was their
visual androgyny, the Beatles wigs that went on sale being
the market leaders in a range of products that included lunch-
boxes, wallpaper, and stockings. The Beatles were like living
dolls, lovable mop-tops packaged for a "passive" female
consumer, yet their long hair contained messages that would
be liberating to both men and women. The truism is that they
arrived in America as a deus ex machina, to fill the gaping
void caused by President Kennedy's assassination in November 1963—the first real failure of the postwar American
dream—but they also arrived as the result of a long social
process. The Beatles announced nothing less than the postwar
baby boomers seizing their time: hereafter the world would

have to bend to *their* desires, and would have to be seen through *their* eyes. In England, this was expressed through style; in the America of the time, this was expressed in politics.

In the fifties, there had been no broad counterculture to the middle-class conformity demanded by deep, Cold War fears of communism and desired as the delayed result of their labors by the wartime generation. Although Abe Peck locates the first cracks in this conformity as early as 1954[49]—the year that McCarthy was censured by the Senate, a "diplomatic miscue" was made in Vietnam, and the Supreme Court ruled that "'separate but (un)equal' education of the races was illegal"—any differing images or social movements were quickly marginalized by the dominant culture. America was still class-based: the era of the teenager who related to other teenagers across class, as a youth community, had not yet arrived. Rock 'n' roll was a subterranean, working-class culture: its products did not theorize, and within a couple of years, had either found God or been packed into the army and off the airwaves. In the same way, affiliated film stars, like Brando or Dean, were framed by scripts that were "tracts for middle-class conformity: grow up, settle down, and if necessary, betray the old, delinquent gang on your way up to more acceptable circles."[50]

Beatniks were the first middle-class involvement with, as opposed to consumption of, the new teenage presence. Contemporary participants like John Clellon Holmes believed that the Beats articulated the "rebellious spirit represented by rock 'n' roll, dope addiction, juvenile delinquency, an amoral attitude toward sex," and urged America's emotional grown-ups to take heed. Brought to public attention by the extraordinary 1957 success of Jack Kerouac's *On the Road,* the Beats had, for the ten years previously, "hung out in a demimonde inhabited by drifters, junkies, male prostitutes, thieves, would-be poets, and actual musicians." The Beats acted out the existential, present tense of the new psychic map, both in their

life and their work: in this respect, Kerouac's voluble romanticism and William Burroughs' austere, accelerated time zones
were cast from the same mold. Socially, they cast further light
on the still dimly-illuminated shadows; intellectuals from the
lower-middle class, "they spoke from an underclass of unassimilated people to an unassimilated corner of the middle-
class psyche."

There was also a new political assertiveness among the
middle-class, affiliated to but not resulting from the Beat rebellion. In 1959, as Abe Peck notes, University of California
President Clark Kerr said: "The employers will love this generation. They aren't going to press many grievances. . . .
There aren't going to be any riots."[51] The next year, there
were the first organized demonstrations from students on the
Berkeley campus, the starting point from which the Free
Speech struggle would grow, and a new broad cultural movement—Students for a Democratic Society—offered a vision of
a New Left that connected "everything from nuclear war to
mass-produced boredom [a future situationist line] to 'partici-
patory democracy.'" That same year, four black students from
a North Carolina college "began the sixties" by insisting on
service at a segregated lunch counter. Civil rights dominated
the political agenda from the early beginnings of the movement in 1955; by 1963, "two hundred thousand demonstra-
tors, black and white together, surrounded the reflecting pool
between the Lincoln Memorial and the Washington Monu-
ment." This political visibility was paralleled by a growing
cultural visibility and a new economic assertion on behalf of
blacks. After the success of Sam Cooke—his "You Send Me"
was the number one pop single in 1957—and Ray Charles—
whose "What'd I Say" went to number six pop in 1959—the
American charts featured a trickle, slow but sure, of unalloyed
emotional rhythm and blues—later called "soul"—and the
more sophisticated, urban sound of the girl group style. By
the mid-sixties, Berry Gordy had fused the two into the Motown dance factory, the first great black American commercial
success story.[52]

The Beatles thus alerted a generation becoming aware of its power. Their unprecedented success brought new wealth into the music industry in particular—1964 was a boom year for record sales both in America and in England—and the teenage industries in general. The prophecies of early teenage proselytizers like Gilbert and Abrams were coming true beyond their wildest dreams: the teenager was now firmly established as a discrete category of consumer with a generational rather than a class definition, and with a pole position in the marketplace that began to confer social power. This was quickly tested by the event that skewered the youth culture of the mid-sixties into real politics—in America at least —and gave it its urgency: the Vietnam War. Late in 1961, U.S. combat troops had arrived in Vietnam; after the assassination of President Diem in 1963, the war between North and South Vietnam became "Americanized," and in 1965 the draft was introduced for all males from 18 to 25. The very real threat of being pulverized in a war that, from 1965 on, was being shown in full color on television, mobilized a generation. By October of that year the first draft card was burned and over one hundred thousand people demonstrated against the war in forty cities. Vietnam marked the arena for a struggle between the "aggressive masculinity kept fervently alive by two decades of Cold War anticommunism" and a new sensibility that believed that "some masculine demiurge, latent perhaps in all men, had simply run amok." As Barbara Ehrenreich observes, "masculinity itself would have to lose status."[53]

The intense commercial and social pressure put on pop— as the cutting edge of the new youth culture—resulted in a fast-moving interchange of styles and ideas across the Atlantic and a thorough acting out of the messages coded within the new English package. In this, long hair was the key, as the Barbarians noted in their 1965 stomper, "Are You a Boy or Are You a Girl": "You're either a gurl . . . or you come from Liverpool!" Worlds fused as the social and political trends that had been gestating in comparative isolation during the previous decade came together.[54] The Rolling Stones—with the Beatles, the leaders of the new pop aristocracy—sold to white Americans a blaring, punk version of the black music they'd never heard; not only were they very fashionable but, for a brief period in 1966, very uptown. A similar social mobility was mirrored at Andy Warhol's East 47th Street Factory, where Pop Art met pop, where the influential and the rich— like heiress Edie Sedgwick—mixed with hustlers, transsexuals, and "A-heads," all fueled by endless amounts of amphetamine. Bob Dylan shed his "movement" credentials and took beatnik poetry and existentialism right into the heart of pop culture with a series of brilliant, evocative records. On the West Coast, the Byrds took Dylan's existentialism further into a religious, Jungian drone where not only gender, but the nature of perception itself became blurred.

This happened with dazzling speed. The sensibility is well described in *Edie*: "It promised a good life without any tomorrow. You really believed that you were going to travel in this bubble right out to the end of the stratosphere. You weren't going to have to cope with the normal structures of life and getting older and making a living."[55] Youth culture was turning into a youth utopia: by the end of 1966, the fusion of drugs, sexual, social, and political forces led baby boomers to confuse purchasing power with political power. In the messianic fervor of the emerging hippie movement, structuring an "alternative" world—if not actually taking the world over— did seem like a possibility. One particular record and the film that accompanies it, an early pop video, catches the teenager at the crossroads. The Rolling Stones' "Have You Seen Your Mother, Baby, Standing in the Shadow" is a nihilist blast of noise ten years ahead of its time, a confused, compressed dredging up of chaos and disturbance from out of the collective psyche. Peter Whitehead's film amplifies the song's sexual and social threat in an editing pattern of cut-ups that mirrors the sensibility of the time. There are two run throughs; in the first, the Stones invoke a riot at an English concert; in the second, they dress up in drag for a Jerry Schatzberg photo-call. Performance shots and New York street scenes are inter-cut with dervish girls, startling images of gender blurring, and the manic, Pan laughter of Brian Jones. The message is clear and yet oddly ambiguous: we are all enveloped by the shadows. Inverted, this is the paranoid dream of *Invasion of the Body Snatchers* come to life: we are *all* aliens now.

The hippie culture that developed in America during 1966 and 1967—and that then spread throughout the world—rep-resents youth culture at its period of greatest outreach. Hippies took a mass bohemianism—a concentration on the moment, on pleasure—into the heart of western culture; "acting out what the Beats wrote," their androgyny held implicit "a new consciousness, [which] takes note that our society has become overbalanced in favor of the so-called masculine qualities of character." [56] Yet this youth culture reached its point of greatest influence at the very moment of its decline. This was partly due to the nature of its experience: the problem with the moment is that it doesn't last and, as June Singer has observed, "wholeness is not achieved, for frenzy is not free-dom." The spirituality of the mid-sixties, while far-reaching, can also be seen as fragile and neurotic: as the maverick polemicist Christopher Booker wrote, "the constant search for novelty and sensation had finally consumed everything but itself. Behind the glittering dreamworld facade, behind the pounding sound track . . . the frenzy of nervous energy in all directions, lay nothing but dust." [57] The teenager's moment was not based on real structures but the wishful thinking caused by a rush of possibility: as the social and political factors on which it was predicated changed, it became vul-nerable.

It is hard to imagine now, but the very blithe confidence of the hippies—that the world was theirs—marked them as a real threat: the famous October 1967 march on the seat of the American military machine, the Pentagon, marked an in-creasing social polarization caused by the deepening war in

Vietnam. The paranoid sweep of teen takeover movies like
*Wild in the Streets* or *Privilege* was quickly superseded by real
events. In 1967, the arrest and subsequent brief jailing of two
Rolling Stones on flimsy drug charges became an English
cause célèbre; it highlighted what was to become commonplace—the institutional harassment of pop stars. In May
1968, the student riots in Paris nearly brought down the De
Gaulle government and inspired imitations throughout Europe. And, in 1967 and 1968, America cracked wide open:
black riots in Newark and Detroit; the assassinations of Martin
Luther King and Bobby Kennedy; the extraordinary violence
that occurred during the 1968 Democratic Convention in Chicago. As the result of any one of these events—or, as is more
likely, a combination of them all—the great American postwar dream of a new society—which had inspired all this
youth activity in the first place—turned sour. Where the dy-
namo of youth culture had been, there was a sudden void.

The vision of a youth utopia quickly faded, its demise
marked by a series of much-publicized deaths and disasters.
In its wake, the complex politics that had informed it splin-
tered into a variety of more specific, enduring political movements. In America, blacks became more militant and more
separatist. Youth androgyny was more fully explored by the
Women's Movement that emerged in the early seventies: the
new, more radical feminists didn't indict "a nameless system
that spanned psychoanalysis, advertising, and suburban architecture," they "blamed *men*, and popularized a whole vo-
cabulary of male faults—sexism, male chauvinism,
misogyny."[58] In a similar process, the 150 or so homophile
groups active in the United States became a more focused
movement after the Stonewall Riots in June 1969. In the rhetoric of the "youth revolution," homosexuals asserted a new
visibility and self-confidence marked by the new description,
"gay."

Once its politics had been hived off, existing commercial
structures moved to accommodate youth culture styles and

sensibilities. The music industry, for instance, now had enough money and experience to handle even the most re-calcitrant hippies: the signing of the San Francisco groups to major record companies for large advances merely confirmed the industry's power.[59] Despite some hiccups, the sixties generation of musicians firmed up music industry structures and practices, like FM radio, which still pertain today; many of them have their reward by remaining on the charts. Most tellingly, the hippie sensibility—instant pleasure, transcendence—was *trained* to adapt to the old therapeutic ethos that had been one of the foundations of American capitalism. As Barbara Ehrenreich notes, "in the pursuit of pleasure, hippiedom did not so much counter the mainstream culture, as anticipate it, magnify it to transcendent proportions, and enrich it."[60] The teens won, but they took over at exactly that point at which they lost their idealism: the result is a consumer society based on the teenage sensibility—a "perpetual present" and "perpetual change"[61]—that is part dream, part nightmare. Infinitely graded and sophisticated, this society is still dominated by that brief but explosive period in the mid-sixties whose implications (and detritus) live with us still.

# TRAPPED IN HISTORY

**The big Beatles year of 1987, in which both the twentieth anniversary of the legendary album *Sgt. Pepper's Lonely Hearts Club Band* and the twenty-fifth anniversary of the group's signing to EMI records and its first single "Love Me Do" are being celebrated, gets underway in fine style with the first official release of the Beatles' music on compact disc.[62]**

All meaning and every goal having disappeared, it becomes possible to wander through civilizations as if through vestiges and ruins. The whole of mankind becomes an imaginary museum: where shall we go this weekend, visit the Angkor ruins or take a stroll in the Tivoli of Copenhagen? We can very easily imagine a time close at hand when any fairly well-to-do person will be able to leave his country indefinitely in order to taste his own national death in an interminable aimless voyage.[63]

It is now clear that the sensibility and success of commercial youth culture were harbingers of the economic and cultural state described as postmodernist; the psychic states that were once the province of deviants or marginals are now at the heart of the Western consumer machine. Postmodernism—a term borrowed from architecture and aesthetic theory—is an attempt to define a new cultural and economic totality, hegemony even, that, as Pat Aufderhide notes, "is marked by several distinctive features. Among them are the merging of commercial and artistic image production, and an abolition of traditional boundaries between an image and its real-life referent, between past and present, between character and performance, between mannered art and stylized life." Postmodernism's "everlasting present" leads it to "obliterate traditions of the kind which all earlier social formations have had in one way or another to preserve."[64] One way in which this is expressed in perception is through the now constant rewriting of history in the language of the present, and nowhere is this seen more clearly than in pop culture, that once most modernist of media which is now drowning in its own past.

The famous 1986 Levi's campaign is a good case in point. This TV advertisement, shown on both sides of the Atlantic, showed a young man—with a fifties DA topping the perfect body—walking into a launderette in an unspecified present from any time within the last thirty years (bearing in mind, as does David Lynch's vertiginous "Blue Velvet," that the fifties fashions worn by the young women could be fifties retro). To the strains of "I Heard It Through the Grapevine"—a 1968 "classic" meant to signify taste, authenticity, and the community of a shared past—the young man strips to his boxer shorts and basks in the gaze of the male and female onlookers. "Look at me," he says, "but don't touch. I don't *need* you." As a Levi's spokesperson notes, "The campaign captures the atmosphere of the 1950s in a 1980s style, effectively 'air-conditioning' the past and achieving a dramatic and compelling crossover of image, music, and fashion."[65] Not only did the campaign do its job of selling jeans—sales went up by a claimed eight hundred percent in the U.K.[66]—but it became a genuine cultural artifact: its "star," Nick Kamen, parlayed himself into a U.K. Top 10 hit from the ad's notoriety, while two subsequent Levi's ads in the same genre resulted in their "featured" songs, Ben E. King's 1961 "Stand By Me" and Percy Sledge's 1966 "When A Man Loves A Woman," reaching number one and number two respectively, on the English charts.

With hindsight, the clip's extraordinary success lies in its summation of recent cultural and industrial trends, the ultimate importance of advertising not as a means to an end, but as an end in itself. These days, in the circularity that is postmodernism's queasy motion, ads advertise ads. In its "tired old visual arrogance,"[67] the Levi's ad holds true to fashion advertising's central tenet, yet it is nonetheless innovative: although the commercial use of "classic" hits is ubiquitous, rarely is it employed so tastefully, in such a seamless fusion of the pulling power of pop and sex. Meticulously researched —its "period detail" is as lavish as any of the feature films, pop videos, or period TV dramas with which it is competing —the Levi's clip is a perfect simulacrum of teenage history: its deliberate anachronisms—which highlight the difference between the historical and the fictional fifties—show how much things have changed between then and now. Their primacy in the clip swamps any documentary reading, which is deliberate: the past now has no use value except in terms of the present, and it is in the nature of postmodernism that the simulacrum is real.

The most obvious anachronism—late sixties song in late fifties setting—is easily explained: the song made famous by Marvin Gaye—so faithfully rerecorded in the ad that you don't realize that it's not the "original"—is there because it's part of the accepted canon of teenage taste. Like Savile Row, it's a timeless badge of quality. It accords too with recent cross-media use of sixties black American music to suggest cool, hipness, and community to a white audience insecure about such qualities. More to the point, however, is the Levi's model and his location. From the neck up, Kamen's sallow pout makes him a dead ringer for any late fifties Elvis clone —say, Frankie Avalon—but this is mere detail: the point of the ad is his model's body, which is both "masculine"—well-formed, with all the right bits in the right places—and "feminine"—displaying the passivity of the adored object. Within the terms of reference of the historical fifties, this crosses codes confusingly: the Frankies of that time didn't have bodies like that—being poor, Italian-American war babies—and the men who did would neither display them like that in public nor expect such adoration. Kamen's narcissistic, androgynous exclusivity is very 1980s. In the historical fifties, no doubt he'd have been attacked as some kind of faggot by the "regular folks" who are extras in the ad. This doesn't make the fifties any better, but it does show the extent to which those qualities that were once derided are now at the center of the consumer stage.

In his early twenties, Kamen is chronologically within the classic teenage age. On the face of it, his easy domination of this prime cultural product seems like a victory for the teenage principle—and the social processes, which it represents—but that has changed as well: "As elsewhere in twentieth-century cultural history, images of autonomy obscure its eclipse."[68] The Levi's ad is not a teenage product, although it's partly aimed at teenagers: its prime orientation is toward a newly-defined, consumer group, usually called yuppies or baby boomers. During the last five years, a new "life-style" marketing fantasy has supplanted the postwar teenage dream: instead of the former 15-to-24 age group, it is now the 25-to-45-year-olds who are being heavily targeted. The *1986 Yearbook of the British Phonographic Industry* spells out the reasoning: "The record industry, confronted by the twin threat of youth unemployment and the declining number of teenagers, will need to direct its marketing strategies accordingly."[69] This fantasy, like the teenage fantasy, has its basis in demographics: both in England and America, the bulk of the sixties baby boomers are passing through their teenage right now, and from now until the end of the century, the 25-to-45-year-olds will be increasing. This age bracket is employed, often "upscale," and has already been trained to consume in the period of the teenage's greatest outreach. The consumers of those products marked teenage in the commodity marketplace are now, as the nostalgic references of the Levi's ad illustrate, not teenaged but middle-aged.

The easy androgyny of the Levi's ad could be taken, then, to mark the full working out of the ideas and ideals of the sixties. Nick Kamen's image is, nevertheless, the result of a complicated process: the successful "life-style" marketing[70] of health filtered through elements of homosexual style and sensibility for a heterosexual, male consumer. In this respect, homosexuality has "moved from the margins to the center" in several ways. The "camp" sensibility whose gay origins were first explored by Christopher Isherwood in 1954's *The World in the Evening* has become an intimate informant of postmodernist style. Defined by Susan Sontag in her keynote 1964 essay as "one way of seeing the world as an aesthetic phenomenon, not in terms of beauty but in terms of the degree of artifice, of stylization." Camp was a metaphorical device for dealing with, and expressing, the disguise and alienation that were part of the homosexual life-style until the mid-sixties. Brilliantly exploited by Andy Warhol—in his Pop Art, and through the Factory milieu—it spread to pop from the late sixties on, most noticeably in the U.K. through the made-up, theatrical style later called glam rock, best exemplified by David Bowie's bitchy *Ziggy Stardust* (1972) and the Sweet's *Ballroom Blitz* (1973).

The tacky shimmer of lurex flouncing now looks primitive. Camp has become an all-pervasive ingredient in a pop culture (so much so that it's not called camp anymore[71]) whose postmodernist style is full of artifice and is carefully constructed, even at that point where, like Bruce Springsteen, it is exaggeratedly "real." References abound to pop's past, as the shared pool of teenage taste and teenage history become part of the novelty. Pop and its culture have become reified, ironicized, once-removed from the fundamental impulses that called it into being. In America, this has been marked by the influence of MTV and its vacant visual codes—signifying everything but meaning nothing, in a closed loop—or the actual integration, through new computer technology, of obsolete music samples into new forms.[72] In England, it has been marked by a ten-year style delirium. Ever since punk took clothing from every subculture since the war, ripped it up, and put it back together with safety-pins, postwar English youth styles have been revived and now coexist in a serial dance.[73] What was once a process is now a costume.

As it moves further away from essentials into commodities, late consumer capitalism demands an even greater "freedom of choice"; in effect, this means a greater gradation of products—cars might *look* the same but they come in ten variants, with twenty optional extras—and a new emphasis on the pleasure of interpretation. The Levi's ad thus comes coded with references that are pleasurable to the desired 25-to-45-year-old male; it also, quite literally, draws on ideas of disguise—as Nick Kamen pulls off the jeans to reveal . . . polka dot boxers—familiar in gay subculture for well over fifty years. The static image of the heterosexual male—if you look at any ad from the forties or fifties, men are displayed with reference either to their status (businessman, paterfamilias) or to some activity (preferably golf or fishing)—has been replaced by a more fluid, less obviously macho man ready to take on any number of identities in heroic consumption. Here, the costumes of the teenager are waiting on the rack.

The market prototype for this feminized New Man is to be located in the gay subculture of the early seventies: after they had "sorted themselves out from the straights," gay men perceived themselves not only as a subculture but as an "alternative" society. Vital to this was an idea of sex as pure, free-floating pleasure that seemed like a real liberation from the religious restrictions (whether Puritan or Catholic) that were endemic in America and England; this particular sexuality was also attractive because it was, as any visitor to a gay disco will attest, so finely intertwined with consumption. The visible symbol of this sexuality was a concentration on the body, first made perfect and then, by the end of the seventies, hardened into the macho "clone" look. The body itself was turned into an easily selected, off-the-rack sex product.

This gay *détournement* of traditional masculine codes freed heterosexuals from the ultimate sanction against feminization: just because they softened up a bit or took some care with their appearance didn't necessarily make them gay anymore. It also liberated certain elements of the gay life-style that had clashed with the newly-desired narcissism, as male vanity became big business. Ever since the fifties, the "Type A," traditional American male—whose qualities included "extremes of competitiveness, striving for achievement, aggressiveness"—had been under attack from a variety of forces: from the beatniks' refusal, from sixties androgyny, from the very desires of men themselves. The striking rhetorical success of the Women's Movement and feminism from the late sixties evinced a male reply, Men's Liberation. At first, as

Barbara Ehrenreich notes, "it was in part a sincere attempt to respond to feminism, but it was also the old male revolt in new guise."[74] This old male revolt was the simple desire not to take on the responsibility of a female dependent and a family: as the seventies wore on, this desire became enshrined in middle-class values, where "health was linked to class status, and both in turn were linked to a movement away from the rigidity of the breadwinner's role." In this light, Nick Kamen's unavailability is not mere narcissism, but the index of a male exclusivity given the commercial seal of approval.

The effect of the sixties on sexuality has, in short, been "real and pervasive,"[75] which accounts for the strength of the reaction against them. If international communism and the labor movements were "the embodiment of absolute evil for an earlier generation of the right," today it is "feminism and homosexuality,"[76] both of which have become more vulnerable through the very process of definition and separation that has marked their success. The spread of AIDS since the early eighties has been a perfect index of this, providing an excellent platform for the rise of a harsh New Right morality. And nowhere is the fundamentalist theory behind the New Right more obvious than in their obsessive condemnation and policing of young people (given that the products of youth culture have always had a quasi-religious function, it is not surprising that this reaction has had a distinctly religious flavor). But the increasing influence of the various censorship lobbies and "parent" groups is less important than the way their terror of "illicit" sexual pleasure is now being coded into pop culture itself, as part of its own history.

A good example is the current (April 1988) U.K. Levi's ad, which continues in the Nick Kamen tradition of being a market leader. At under a minute, the ad purports to tell the "real" story of how Sharon Sheeley met Eddie Cochran in (as the opening caption reads) "New York, New Year's Eve, 1958." This puts it within the bio-pic discourse of *La Bamba*, whose title track, performed by Los Lobos, was a number one hit on both sides of the Atlantic in 1987. "Somethin' Else," the Eddie Cochran song featured here as sound track, in the circular motion typical to these ads, went to number fifteen in the U.K. on its re-release in February 1988.

Spin-offs aside, the very thrust of the ad is peculiar. Basically, our Sharon is behaving like a groupie: "how to get to Eddie," she moons dreamily while writhing on her bed. Except that by the time she's put on her sweatshirt and Levi's jeans she looks dressed for Sunday School. Despite the fact that the ad's pulling power is sex, she is curiously virginal, a quality shared by the "shopping mall" generation of girl teen stars like Debbie Gibson and Tiffany. The total lust lack of these paragons is a classic post-AIDS fudge: how to use sex to sell your product when the very audience you're trying to reach is the target of specific government health warnings against sex (in the U.K., at least). Add to this the ad's generally necrophilic aspect—in common with Ritchie Valens, Cochran was an early, very public rock 'n' roll fatality—and you have an implicit equation: Youth and/or Sex = Death.

This ad marks a new stage in youth culture's necrosis, where an authoritarian morality does not, as previously thought, have to clash with the amorality of the free market. Youth is no longer vital to capital, and its freedoms are being curtailed: like gays have been, youth is now on the "frontline" of AIDS and beginning to bear the burden of the new restrictive morality. Faced by a double disenfranchisement—from both sex and power through consumption—many young people can't wait to become like their more fortunate elders, those middle-aged teenagers, hence a move towards more conservative, docile styles dictated by the older age group. The corollary is a near total alienation, where the fact that youth suicide has tripled during the last twenty-five years gives an unpleasant gloss on the canonization of dead but permanently young and cute rock stars.

This removal of youth's power has been heralded by a

fresh series of restrictions placed upon all minorities. This is an explicit New Right project against pluralism: among those attacked in Britain since the early eighties are the traditional working class (the miner's strike of 1984), blacks, and especially gays, who now occupy the place of public bogeymen. This represents the success of the New Right's exploitation of AIDS as a powerful agent of fear: as AIDS spreads to heterosexuals in the U.K., gays are isolated and "blamed," to the extent that explicitly antigay legislation—section 28 of the Local Government Bill, which prevents any local council from "promoting" homosexuality—became law in April 1988.

Traditional morality here operates with the new dynamic of commodity capitalism toward *exclusion*: it is brutally clear that the majority is simply superfluous to the new economy, provided that a few can consume to the point of gluttony. This is the end of consumption's democratic project begun in the early years of this century: as pop becomes more and more integrated with advertising—part of the colonizing thrust of multinational media industry—it has nothing left to offer to those out-groups that it once enfranchised.

The walls are going up. Inside, behind the barbed wire, security systems, and searchlights is the baby-boomer oligarchy, brought up with a teenage model of consumption that may well be obsolete. Outside, the excluded, waiting for admittance or baying at the moon. With the quickening collapse of our ecosystem, a critique of this model of consumption is urgently needed: it is ironic that those with the most power to take action are those whom it has most tainted.

# M<sup>c</sup>
# R
# O
# C
# K

*Pop as a*

*commodity*

I have in front of me a memo, dated May 16, 1967, from the office of the vice president of the American Broadcast Company Merchandising Inc. The memo, which a friend of a friend found lying forgotten in a filing cabinet some fifteen years after it was written, was never implemented, but I like to feel that it contains within its pages some of the eternal spirit of the music business.

The memo is titled "BUGALU (Exploitation)." Written at the height of the media explosion over youth culture, and reflecting the eager bewilderment of corporate executives faced with a new era, it suggests a campaign to create and market a new music movement that would be tailored for the new youth audience. The music was to be called (after a mid-sixties dance craze) "bugalu."

**From our preliminary discussion, we are agreed on the overall purpose, which is to popularize the word BUGALU.**

It is the intent to make the word synonymous with the
PURPOSES of the Young World. We are agreed that the
Young, to date, have borrowed expressions, slogans,
methods and have no such which has been derived FROM
WITHIN THEMSELVES. Such expressions as "mod," "in,"
"happening," etc., are as much a part of the adult world
as in the Young vernacular.

The plan, then, is to establish a word as the rallying
point for their own ideas and identities . . . a word that
signifies what they're trying to do with themselves and
the world in general—their outlook, their frame of mind,
their goals. . . .

This idealistic plan for the American Broadcasting Corpo-
ration to create a spontaneous youth culture vernacular was
to be implemented through colleges, using student represen-
tatives and with the deployment of certain heroes of the youth
movement:

The acknowledged "leader" of this movement of
Revolution and Evolution is Allen Ginsberg. When he
speaks, the others pick up the thread and follow. Despite
the references to him as a "kook," his acceptance by the
young is undisputed; he speaks for them. He is more
aware of the rise of LOVE, than anyone else and currently
is starting to spread the gospel on the West Coast—(from
whence comes most of the impetus to Youth movements).
It would pay to have Ginsberg contacted, the purpose
explained, and—if he agrees—to pay him a fee to write
and recite a poem embodying the word and its meaning.
This is like putting a match to a fuse: Ginsberg talks, they
listen.

The fuse was never lit, and the great bugalu campaign
remained a dream lost in a filing cabinet. Rock music has
always lived within the tension between spontaneous popu-

lar eruption and corporate control, and, as this glorious memo shows, we should never underestimate the music industry's capacity to get it all wrong.

We call the aggressive marketing of pop trends "hype," and for most critics hype is a dirty word: this is the bad side of popular music, the false glitter that is used to seduce an innocent public away from truer and more authentic forms of musical experience. Or so some critics would tell us, implying that there is a living folk art smothered by the wickedness of record companies and MTV. But as the bugalu memo proves, record companies don't always find it so easy to manipulate the public. And in any case, what is authentic music in an age of mass media? And how can we disassociate pop from hype, when the two have been entwined from the beginning? Hype may be tawdry, but without it pop would lose much of its urge to live. The lust for glory, the scheming for quick money and quick fame are all part of pop music's vitality, and have been ever since Elvis Presley went after his first gold suit.

# DREAM LOVERS

In the 1950s, no one had any doubt that pop was hype. The whole adult world saw it as a huge confidence trick foisted upon gullible teens, in which any idiot with the right pompadour and no talent could be yanked off the streets and turned into a star. This was the image of pop presented by Stan Freberg on record when he parodied "Sh-boom," and looking at the career of Fabian you can see the point (not that anyone had great illusions about Fabian's talents, least of all the boy himself, for this was in the days before pop singers had become artists with a vision and a reputation to uphold).

All that was required of a teen idol was that he be cute and mildly sultry, offering sex appeal within a clean-cut collegiate mode.

Ironically, most of the stars of the time came from poor ethnic backgrounds and, far from going to college, had spent their youth in street harmony groups hanging around garages and subway stations. The most influential pop publicist of the time, Connie de Nave, was employed by these singers' managers or record companies to make them presentable. One of her tasks was to teach her clients how to read a menu and order a meal in a restaurant, because most of the kids could only ask for hamburgers if they were taken out.

De Nave also vetted every photograph, for if a pop star was shown with a drink or a cigarette in their hand it could mean the end of their career. When her charges had an interview to do she sat with them to monitor the conversation, although she says "I kept my mouth shut. The kids knew what they had to talk about. This was not the press of today: there were only fan magazines. You had to fight to get any space in a newspaper because that was considered a hard news area."[1]

All a pop publicist in the late fifties and early sixties could work with were the newspaper gossip columns, which were oriented toward more traditional show business—nightclub singers, Broadway stars—and the new teen magazines, which were largely modeled on the old movie fan mags. Because they had no competition from the mainstream these magazines acquired tremendous power, and the most successful, Gloria Stavers' *Sixteen,* could break a new act simply by printing a photo spread. So if the publicist's territory was smaller than it is today it was also easier to manipulate: the fan magazines and the publicists recognized their mutual need, and this tacit understanding kept unseemly photographs and news stories out of print.

Operating on a rigid format, the teen magazines reduced every story to a dreamy sameness. All pain and deprivation and dangerous habits dropped away; all performers became bright-eyed, personable, and polite. The profiles with their questionnaires about favorite colors and what-do-you-look-for-in-a-girl (answer: personality) offered a cartoon outline of character. The teen idols were fictional characters—they often seemed to be the *same* character—inhabiting a soft, secure, teenage fantasy world.

The marketing of the teen idol has changed very little over the past thirty years, and today a copy of *Star Hits* covers much the same territory as the first issues of *Sixteen* or *Tiger Beat*. Now, however, this marketing is used only for those relatively innocuous acts suited to the young teen female market. Twenty-five years ago all pop acts, however unsuitable, had to go through this one channel and it would take time for the media to develop new outlets to cope with the changes in pop culture. The early sixties were notable for the diversity of teen music, from the Phil Spector stable to surf music to the Brill Building to early Tamla/Motown to the British invasion; yet all acts were marketed in the same way. They appeared on the same television shows, shared the bill on the same package tours, and talked to the same fan magazines. And whether they were from a Detroit slum, a Los Angeles suburb, or the backstreets of Liverpool, their interviews ended up sounding identical.

What the teen magazine audience required was not detailed character analysis but dream material (the photographs) and certain kinds of information (physical characteristics, likes and dislikes, some past history). If the characters appeared too real, too flawed, they could no longer function as dreams. But as pop became more overtly sexual and more consciously rebellious, something had to give. A magazine like *Sixteen* could not radically extend its format without destroying its identity: new channels would have to open up to accommodate the cultural changes that began to emerge in the mid-sixties.

For Connie de Nave it was the Rolling Stones who first

signaled the changing times. By 1964 they had already begun to inspire their own demonology in Britain. De Nave needed to create a rival to the Beatles in America, and as no one could match the Beatles in lovability, she decided to sell the Stones as the band parents would hate. She put out a press release beginning, "The Rolling Stones, who do not believe in bathing, will be visiting New York. . . ." The *New York Times* printed a hostile news story, teenage fans (with much encouragement from de Nave) made a demonstration in the group's favor, and the bandwagon started rolling. The Rolling Stones had started their career in Britain playing R&B cover versions in blues and jazz clubs, but there was one crucial difference between them and the other "purist" performers: the Stones (or at least Mick Jagger, Brian Jones, and Keith Richard) were cute. Whatever their musical roots, their looks and style allowed them to operate commercially on teen idol territory, and in July 1965 it was perfectly natural for Keith Richard—who only two or three years later would be a byword for rock decadence—to be interviewed by the pop magazine *Fabulous* on "My Kind of Girl" ("I get very restless, so I like a girl with plenty of go who will fall in with the mad things I feel like doing"). But despite all this cuteness, when the Stones sang about love it was obvious they meant an adult sexuality, and they began injecting something disturbing into the world of the teen dream.

The pivotal year in the change from innocent pop hype to something more knowing and self-conscious was 1967. Probably the most accurate account of that time is to be found in the back pages of *Billboard;* the magazine has always spoken to the industry and the industry cannot afford to lie to itself. You could almost tell the story of 1967 just through the publicity photographs that hopeful young acts placed in the magazine. The January 21 issue shows that the British invasion was still carrying on its assault, and young American acts were still imitating Carnaby Street style: beefy young men with the look of high-school football stars squeezing themselves into flounced shirts and slicking their hair down over their foreheads in imitation of the Brian Jones dandy look. However, a small ad at the bottom of one page offers a hint of the future, and it does not belong to Britain: "The Peanut Butter Conspiracy Is Coming!" Look at the magazine a few months later, and pop music is in a different world. By May, *Billboard*'s pages were filled with art nouveau graphics, beefy young men were growing their hair past their shoulders and learning the flute, and *Billboard*, stolid old *Billboard*, was carrying ads for posters celebrating hashish.

In 1967, mods turned into hippies and pop into rock, but it was also the first time that certain moral dilemmas surfaced. These were dilemmas about commercialism, "selling out," and what pop music really stood for, and the way those issues were dealt with would affect the way both the music and its industry would develop from then on.

This was the year the pop audience began to take itself and its idols seriously. The process had already begun during the British invasion, but almost imperceptibly so: the little girls who stuck pictures of the Beatles and the Stones on the wall were operating on the same basic territory as Dion's fans. Their parents still regarded them as victims of some ghastly but relatively harmless consumer fraud, while they stood up for the right to dress in the style and listen to the music that they pleased. Pop music was just one element in the battle of the generations over pleasure and free time. In San Francisco, however, the teenagers who were getting out of their heads at the Avalon ballroom saw themselves and their music quite differently. They felt they had stepped outside the bounds of their parents' culture—and of past teenage culture—into a secret world of initiates, sharing in mysteries.

Part of this new hippy culture's raison d'être was that it was not commercial. This was a new generation of bohemians, defining themselves in opposition to the straight world of steady jobs and Madison Avenue and commerce and conformity: the same targets that the bohemians of the fifties had fought against. But this was no coffee house art and poetry movement. Rock music, no matter how weird it might be in San Francisco, was still part of a mass market culture. It defined itself through things—records, posters, clothes, drugs—that were bought and sold. Its liberation from capitalism was always largely illusory, and indeed the most surprising thing to be learned from *Billboard* in 1967 is how quickly and easily the new hippy culture fitted into the existing commercial structure. Far from abandoning hype, the new counterculture simply found different strategies for selling sincerity.

If pop was about buying a dream, rock was about buying an experience. For pop, fun, energy, and glamor are enough; one must be moving when required, but it is not necessary to be "authentic," to sing out of a genuine pain. But in rock conviction matters. In the sixties this was partly due to the legacy of fifties heroes: the great primal rock 'n' rollers like Little Richard and Jerry Lee Lewis on the one hand, and the blues tradition on the other. The sixties rockers admired the deep roots and the powerful emotional quality of their heroes' music and desired not just to reproduce it but to recreate it. In other words, they wanted to experience the emotions that inspired the music in the first place, even though they might be middle-class English boys trying to feel the emotions of black oppression when playing the Delta blues. The test of a song, for these sixties rockers, was in its depth of feeling: how much the performer experienced when playing a song, and how well that experience was transmitted to the audience. But whatever the differences between pop and rock stances, both worked through the same vehicles of records, concerts, and magazines, and both had to be marketed; after all, someone had to pay for the recording costs. The differences, in short, were not between commercial and noncommercial musics, but between attitudes toward commercialism. If pop stars and marketing were seen as indivisible—the fan magazines actually urged their readers to share in celebrating the stars' commercial success by focusing on record sales and chart positions—rock stars needed to be seen as standing outside that process. The most revered of mid-sixties rock stars, Bob Dylan, was worshiped all the more because of his refusal to talk to the press.

The paradox (and the profits) lay in the fact that rock's anticommercialism became the basis of its commercial appeal. Rock fans saw their stars not as commodities but as artists; what they valued was not their sales success but their music, their message, and their daring in opposing the status quo—an opposition that reflected the great divisions in society at large over the war in Vietnam—but such an evaluation still meant buying records (and making heroes). This new rock culture was most obvious in the clubs of San Francisco: for the first time, bohemia spawned a mass culture movement and moved into the marketplace while keeping its values intact. A rock star's integrity (and that of his audience) was defined by his contempt for the old pop hype, a contempt that was matched by the sudden unfashionability of early sixties pop acts, matching suits, publicity stunts, fan mags, and all. It was quickly obvious that rock artists would still have to cooperate with the music industry (as one by one the "countercultural" acts signed their record deals). But from now on the argument was that they were using that industry for their own ends.

And crucial to the argument was the suggestion that stars and fans were somehow in alliance *against* the business that actually mediated between them. This was illustrated by the way in which the bands began to dress like their audiences (rather than vice versa). When the Beatles went hippie in 1967, it was both a gesture of solidarity with the streets and a mark of independence from their record company.

# THE REVOLUTION IS ON CBS

For the music industry it was still business as usual, and it wasn't long after its infancy that the San Francisco scene

was discovered and analyzed in terms of its commercial prospects. The May 6, 1967, edition of *Billboard* contained a special "Spotlight on San Francisco" that included a very sharp
and knowledgeable survey of the local clubs, radio stations,
DJs, managers, and top bands. An article by one of the editors, Eliot Tiegel, outlined both the exciting potential and the
problems inherent in dealing with this new movement:

> **The long-haired, bizarre appearing groups, whose names
> are wildly freakie (many with relationships to drugs,
> insiders whisper) have become the ripe apple in many a
> record company's menu. Unfortunately, many of these
> pop groups aren't giving themselves up for cooking yet.
> They have adopted the "freedom now, love us for our
> inherent talents" concept in their dealings with the
> Establishment (substitute record company official if you
> wish). Probably for the first time, untested, unproven acts
> are standing up to record company labels and saying:
> "Baby, if you want to sign us up, there are a couple of
> things we have to get straight. Like, we want artistic
> control of our product, control of our album covers, and
> we want to name the A&R man. Dig?" Where is the awe
> for the giant record company with its greased and oiled
> A&R, sales, merchandising, and promotion departments?
> In San Francisco among the pop/hippies, it's not too
> overpoweringly evident.**

The San Francisco groups had the three assets needed to
disrupt the music industry: a powerful grassroots following, a
new and original style reflecting the culture that had produced it, and a strong sense of their own importance and
destiny. However, this didn't mean that they spurned the industry, far from it. *Billboard* reported that locally-based labels
like Fantasy had no luck in signing these local groups. Instead, it was the New York and Los Angeles companies who
bought up and had commercial success with the Jefferson

Airplane, Sopwith Camel, Mojo Men, and the Grateful Dead, bidding for the Jefferson Airplane being particularly fierce. Only one young manager, Ron Polte of the Quicksilver Messenger Service, did say that he and his group were waiting for a "hippy label" to be formed. "We're looking for a company that will allow us to go into the studio, record our work unedited, and not change our natural image. We're all waiting for an honest record company that we can talk with." (Quicksilver signed a contract in 1967 with Capitol.)

It was a change in style and attitude, not in structure that he was looking for: a style that would shortly be provided by the development of "hip capitalism" in many laid-back but profit-minded companies. The new hippy culture was by no means independent of the boring old commercial establishment (even if they justified their record deals as a beautiful, alternative way of living), but the fact that they did believe themselves to be independent paradoxically gave these groups a genuine power. They weren't going to sign contracts easily, and *Billboard* reported that in order to woo the San Francisco sound the industry had had to offer "some of the best contracts ever signed by commercially untested acts . . . 5 to 8 percent minimums with substantial side advances."

Naturally, having spotted one such creative and potentially profitable scene, the record industry was tempted to invent another. The result was one of the great failed hypes of the sixties, "The Boss Town Sound," an attempt by MGM Records to set up Boston as an East Coast rival to San Francisco through such immortal groups as Ultimate Spinach. Some pop stars, like the teen idols, can be manufactured from scratch. In the case of the Monkees in the sixties or Menudo in the eighties such stars can even gain from being prefabricated: they are fantasy figures and the knowledge that they were manufactured, like a toy, can simply reinforce the cartoon element of their story. Manufacturing a whole rock movement, though, is something else. The strength of the San Francisco scene had developed slowly, building on a local bohemian tradition and enriching it with various musical crosscurrents. Such a development is haphazard and organic, and cannot be reproduced: this gives the grassroots element in rock the power, at certain key moments, to disrupt seriously the music industry and, at least temporarily, to alter its balance of power. The San Francisco sound in 1967 was one example, the punk scene in London in 1977 was another.

As *Billboard* noted, one effect of the strength of San Francisco's grassroots rock culture was to increase the musicians' confidence and sense of independence, forcing recording contracts to shift in the artists' favor. But in spite of their half-contemptuous attitude toward the music industry, the bands made no serious attempt to move outside it: even when the Jefferson Airplane released their album *Volunteers* with its misty call to revolution, they were still calling from the corporate safety of RCA. This reveals an almost mystic faith in the power of the counterculture, which made things like corporations seem irrelevant. Wherever the new spirit passed it would bring revelation: consciousness would alter, changes would happen, so what did it matter what channels were used to get that spirit across? That was the belief embodied in one of the most naive—and cynical—slogans ever invented by the rock industry, "The Revolution Is on CBS."

The record companies in their turn were confused and even alarmed by the strange groups whose music was so profitable. Faced with a new and uncertain market, they were forced to loosen the reins and bring in young outsiders to tell them what would make a hit. Connie de Nave, who hated the psychedelic era but soldiered on as a press agent, found she no longer recognized the industry she had worked in since the fifties:

**Suddenly, in my business, we had to have house groupies, flower children, who were hired because they were "in." I had one called Tinkerbell working for me. . . . They sat down and talked to the other flower children at**

**Columbia or whatever and they explained to you what was going on.** I stopped making decisions for about two years and relied on my house flower child because she would tell me what was going on in the mainstream—I saw it but didn't understand—and then I would make my judgements on what was going down. This happened at every company. The flower children kind of ran the business for two years.[2]

Why attack the music industry when it is yours to run, when it expresses your every thought—or at least as long as those thoughts sell? (And the disastrous example set by the Beatles when they started their own record company, Apple, discouraged others from venturing outside established companies. They had tried to run a business along hippy lines; it collapsed in chaos.) Only in the early seventies, when the counterculture had lost its politics and its drive, would it become clear how little the corporate structure of the music business had changed. Until then it seemed that the spirit of that culture, channeled through its music, would defeat corporations. Indeed, rock groups didn't actually have to argue much with their record companies at all—as long as their music came out, it was assumed that it would carry all the right oppositional messages (and as long as these messages sold, the record companies didn't argue much about their groups' choice of rhetoric, musical material, record covers, etc.). It was as if everyone was somehow subject to the sheer force of the times.

Jann Wenner reflected this faith in rock music as the natural voice of the counterculture when he wrote, in 1971:

*Rolling Stone* **was founded and continues to operate in the belief that rock 'n' roll music is the energy center for all sorts of changes revolving rapidly around us: social, political, cultural, however you want to describe them. The fact is for many of us who've grown up since World**

War II, rock 'n' roll provided the first revolutionary insight into who we are and where we are at in this country: our first discovery that behind the platicized myth of what we had been told was the United States, behind that Eisenhower-Walt Disney-Doris Day facade was (damn!) a real America: funky, violent, deeply divided, despairing, exultant, rooted in rich historical tradition and ethnic variety. . . .[3]

In 1972 Wenner and Charles Reich, author of *The Greening of America*, co-authored a book on Jerry Garcia (*Garcia: A Signpost to New Space*) with an earnest introduction by Reich —the Yale professor painfully anxious to be part of the hip underground scene—which encapsulated the late sixties vision of rock:

I think there is more truth in rock than in the old Tin Pan Alley hit tunes. Rock is more like the blues, which have been telling the truth for so many years, but for so long spoke only to blacks. Rock deals with sadness, bummers, fear, despair, adversity, desperation, as well as sex, sensuality, highs, and super-highs. The straight world tends to like escapist entertainment, the hip world accepts more pain and thus more reality. If the "new culture" is anything, it is a movement toward greater personal reality.[4]

Obviously, the old teenage publications could not cope with this high seriousness. A new form of pop media developed in the person of the underground press, a loose label for local radical outlets like the *Berkeley Barb* and the *East Village Other*, and the "serious" music magazines like *Crawdaddy, Creem*, and *Rolling Stone*. These publications encompassed the new social and political concerns, registering the new terms of pop freedom in the "greater personal reality" of the star interview. Connie de Nave found that by the late sixties

Fan magazines were out. Instead of teen magazines, light stuff, you had to go into heavier raps, different types of questions: were they mellowing out after a heavy tour, how was the country holding up, did they see anything profound in America? Politics, the spirit of love in the land. Very important information about guitars and their strings. Very important questions about the music. The music was extremely important, so if a guy got a new Martin this would be very heavy and he would give great interviews about it. . . . They would discuss things riff by riff sometimes. But they wouldn't get into stuff about your wife and being on the road, or the money you were making. . . .[5]

## "I'M FROM *ROLLING STONE,* SO IT'S OK"

Sixties rock culture valued honesty, but it valued heroes and their mythology even more, and the media that developed to service it, the music magazines, the FM radio stations, the festivals, were adept myth-makers. It was true that the scope of pop culture had expanded enormously, and these media handled previously X-rated material on sex, drugs, and politics; what they censored, no doubt quite unconsciously, was the mundane side to music, the *Billboard* side. Financial dealings, record company strategy, marketing and publicity campaigns were rarely mentioned; these were irrelevancies, or at worst a corruption of the true spirit of rock 'n' roll.

This was the era of the rock star as genius. The stress on private suffering and the storms of creation, the reverent attention paid to a performer's technique and inspiration, all served to build up a romantic vision of the artist that would have made Shelley blush. It was the old bohemian tradition at work, and that was what the late sixties rock audience had come to expect: moments of ecstasy and upheaval and drama from a music and culture whose whole impetus was to provide an escape from convention.

It was also the era of the rock writer as star. Journalists on the teen magazines had been virtually anonymous, toiling away at the dream factory, producing stories with the barest connection to reality in a uniform house style. But journalists in the underground press were personalities, spokesmen for their generation, and rock stars took them seriously: the rock interview developed from a straight promotions exercise into a freewheeling confessional.

The interview that Ben Fong-Torres did with David Crosby for *Rolling Stone* in 1970 illustrates the contradictory role the rock journalist had developed: half a fan, half a member of the hip elite, discussing chord changes on equal terms with the greats. Fong-Torres begins by reminding his readers of the occasion when Crosby interrupted the Byrds' performance at the Monterey Festival to deliver a "rap" challenging the findings of the Warren Report on the Kennedy assassination. (It is hard these days to put aside the pathetic, drug-blistered image of David Crosby in the 1980s and to remember that in his heyday he was regarded as a kind of friendly god.) Then the tone changes into the rock writer as hipster:

**He said he'd found a journalist he thought he could trust.**
**I'd found a musician-spokesman I knew I could believe.**
**. . . When the tape machine wasn't running, we spent**
**time on the deck of *The Mayan*, docked at Marina del**
**Rey, and talked about London, about women, and about**
**trips he had made in the waters and the winds while he**
**planed and sanded down hatch doors and revarnished**
**various pieces of the boat's woodwork. Downstairs,**

**whenever we talked, friends would invariably gather to listen. . . .**[6]

Once rock stars were morons; now they were oracles. This interview takes in the recent killings at Kent State, the prospects of violent revolution and the state of the Panthers, and the power of the military industrial complex, back to the break up of the Byrds, to Crosby's early life and years in the Sausalito folk scene, to drugs and sex. Money isn't discussed, but the record business is, as Crosby suggests that record companies should release their artists from contracts that bind them to specific groups in favor of a free-floating community of stars:

**I'm certain that for a mutual profit gain these companies can be convinced to allow us to crosspollinate. . . . If somebody takes the trouble to convince them that it'll net 'em twice as much money over the next ten years, we'll get it Tuesday.**[7]

The notion that any record company will abandon its legal contracts is an unlikely one, but it was an optimistic age— and rock stars had never been so rich and so powerful. Crosby was speaking at a time when everything seemed molten, when there was no knowing what strange possibilities—an armed revolution, an entire change in human consciousness —lay just around the corner. Feeding this vision was the sixties' blind faith in the power of youth: youth as the embodiment of man's true, unfallen nature before its corruption by parents, straight culture, and the military-industrial machine. Crosby, explaining his loss of faith in the ability of radical movements to overturn the system says:

**I figured the only thing to do was swipe their kids. I still think it's the only thing to do. By saying that, I'm not talking about kidnapping, I'm just talking about**

changing their value systems, which removes them from
their parents' world very effectively.

And I didn't change 'em, I just offered them an
alternative. On one side you got war, death, degradation,
submission, guilt, fear, competition; and on the other
hand you got a bunch of people lyin' out on the beach,
walkin' around in the sun, laughin', playin' music, makin'
love and gettin' high, singin', dancin', wearin' bright
colors, tellin' stories, livin' pretty easy. Half a million of
'em get together and not even punch one cat out. That's
pretty easy. You offer that alternative to a kid, man, and
the kid ain't crazy yet. The kid ain't had time to be crazy.
He can make a very clear decision about alternatives like
that. I think that they've probably lost the majority of
their kids by now. I don't know frankly. I guess we'll have
to wait and see.[8]

Paul Kantner of the Jefferson Airplane offered a parallel
observation when he said in *Rolling Stone* in 1970 that rather
than using an armed revolution to fight the Establishment, the
only solution was "Stealing their children. 'Cause I don't see
any real hope in changing them. It couldn't be done." If the
children were the future, then rock culture must have time on
its side, the future belonged to the young. Wrapped in this
confidence, and treated like spoiled children by their record
companies, it's not surprising that these stars never thought
very deeply about the industry that supported them. In the
same Jefferson Airplane interview Grace Slick had this to say
about RCA:

So the band makes the music and the tapes go away,
and they come out as records. But RCA is too big even to
refer to. It's like sayin, "Well, how are you dealing with
the government?" I mean, what dealings? You don't deal
with the government at all.

RCA is eight hundred million people with a dollar's

**worth of stock, and there are people doing stuff, like once
every two years we'll meet. Thompson will say, "This is
Joe Heefenbacker, he runs the record division of RCA."
Then he shakes our hands and goes off and does
something. But that particular interchange is
meaningless. It's like walking from one room to another.
You just don't think about it.⁹**

You don't think about it until your records no longer sell.
Record company royalties bought Paul Kantner and Grace
Slick their San Francisco mansion, and record company ads
largely funded the underground press, particularly *Rolling
Stone:* it wasn't just the "revolution" but the manifesto of the
revolution that was on CBS. And by the early seventies, when
it was becoming clear that a transformation in human consciousness was no longer just around the corner and the spirit
of the counterculture had gone flat, the corporate structure of
the music industry—which had always had very little connection with hippy ideals—remained intact.

# WON'T GET FOOLED AGAIN

A t the right cultural moment rock music can have a
remarkable power to create a movement, and at such
moments it seems to need no other dynamic than its own faith
in itself. When that faith falters, it tumbles to earth. By the
early seventies, idealism in rock was a spent force: it had
promised a new utopia and instead delivered hip capitalism
and Crosby, Stills, and Nash. Rock hype, which had been
geared to glamorizing the artist as visionary, rebel, and seer
was still in operation as the record companies offered a series

of minor singer-songwriters as "the new Dylan." But rock romanticism only made sense now as nostalgia, and the rock audience's strongest emotion was reserved for the dead heroes of the sixties—Jimi, Janis, Brian Jones, Jim Morrison—or for those who were now inaccessible like Dylan and John Lennon.

As rock ceased to be the binding force of the counterculture, the rock audience fragmented into separate (and often opposed) groups of fans (heavy metal *versus* disco *versus* adult rock), and star making became a simple matter of applying the right sales formula. With radio dominated by market researched playlists and very little corporate money going to develop new acts, the pop market had never been so conservative or so firmly controlled.

The marketing of teenage music now stressed the remoteness of the rock star rather than countercultural intimacy; the hippy tendency to romanticize the artist was turned into an exaggerated, hysterical star worship in the era of the stadium concert, the supergroup, and the career groupie. But rock could no longer be defined as teenage: it now had an enormous market among those adults who had lived all their rites of passage through rock 'n' roll. When they settled down, so did their music, as the old hippy culture was transformed from a way of life to a "life-style."

Hippies had always had a naive faith in the importance of consumer choice. In his *Rolling Stone* interview David Crosby had asserted, "There are certain key, surface symptoms of value-systems change that you can watch: dress, manner, hair length." And these things did mean something when long hair and a certain kind of dress was enough to indicate which side you were on in Vietnam. By the mid-seventies blue jeans and long hair were not a sign of belief but a matter of taste and, for some, a consolation that they hadn't settled for a dull conformist world.

Nothing illustrated the change in the times as perfectly as *Rolling Stone's* 1977 move from San Francisco, dropping its hippy associations to become a glossy life-style publication— a kind of rock *Esquire*—with a young professional readership. The ads were for expensive stereo equipment, the dominant artists the singer-songwriters who typified the new self-absorption. The one thing that hadn't changed was the seriousness of *Rolling Stone*'s approach to rock, now settled into portentiousness, typified by the ever more weighty star interview that allowed the reader to live through every moment of crisis in James Taylor's life.

Rock in the mid-seventies had reached a crisis similar to that of rock in the mid-sixties: its brand of hype no longer suited the times. The sixties pop crisis was fueled by the emergence of artists and fans who wanted to express themselves rather than simply be entertained. The seventies crisis concerned a music culture that had been created to deliver radical messages but which no longer had anything radical to say. Worse than that, record companies were making their biggest profits ever by *regulating* the urge to be different that had once given rock music its reason to live.

Not surprisingly, cynicism emerged as a dominant creative force. This was the mode favored by the hip rock magazine of the early and mid-seventies, *Creem*. A late 1975 issue of *Creem* is a panorama of confusion, reflecting the splintering of the market: profiles of Steven Stills, Neil Young, and the Eagles ("Fly Me: I'm Vacuous") and the latest updates on Rod Stewart and the Faces rub shoulders with a from-the-bunker report from Lisa Robinson on the new CBGB scene in New York declaring that this "could mark an important change in rock 'n' roll music as we know it today." Yet a definite sensibility emerges, a sensibility that involves a genuine enjoyment of rock's stadium vulgarities while making fun of its stupidities, and which mixes a suspicion of the laid-back California soft rock that now dominated the market with a reverence for the art primitivism of the Velvet Underground and Iggy and the Stooges.

The new mode was irony. It had to be, because once rock

had ceased to believe in its own sales pitch, irony was the only honest stance. "Rock Nihilism," Iggy Pop screaming No Fun!, rock as a deliberately moronic cartoon (the Ramones were stirring in the deep), the New York Dolls' insouciant disregard for musicianship—suddenly all this was progressive. And what was progressive was not mainstream. The search for something new seemed to mean celebrating the unpopular, and it was from this moment on that critical and public taste began to diverge.

With the reversal of accepted rock values came a new assessment of the past. The fifties and early sixties became hip again, as role models of style, energy, and simplicity, and suddenly old-fashioned pop hype seemed exciting too. The publicity stunts, the image making, the fan magazines, the very artificiality seemed more honest than rock's heavy sincerity. (As long as the artificiality was blessed with period charm, of course; no hip rock person was interested in the pop processes of the Osmond Family or the Captain and Tennille).

Sixties rock culture thought it could ignore the sales process, and ended up another commodity. Now a new generation of radicals was determined to embrace that process for its own ends. In contrast to the naïveté of the pop stars of the fifties and sixties, they would bring to it the political consciousness —and the cynicism—left over from the failure of the counterculture: "Won't Get Fooled Again." Sixties rock stars had believed that the truth of their music was something separate from the hype. A new emerging, punk generation said that rock stars were not lonely bohemian artists but mass media figures integrally involved in mass marketing: the truth of their music *was* the hype. Radicalism was possible, as long as it used and exposed that pop process.

The notion of any vital new rock movement emerging in the mid-seventies seemed unlikely all the same. Outrage— which had fueled rock 'n' roll ever since Elvis and Jerry Lee and Little Richard scandalized the suburban values of the 1950s—seemed to be a spent force. What could compete with the sex and drug culture of the sixties, the stadium overkill of the early seventies? When something new finally appeared the industry press treated it, at first, with less trepidation than they had the San Francisco scene in 1967. On October 23, 1976 *Music Week* reported:

**EMI's capture of the Sex Pistols, a group regarded in various quarters as one of the most exciting to have emerged from the wave of new, young British musicians who have generated public and media interest in recent months, was also one of the fastest signings implemented by the company. The act's decision to go to EMI—despite intensive competition from other record firms—was conveyed to A&R manager Nick Mobbs by Pistols manager Malcolm McLaren last Friday morning, and the contract drawn up, checked, and signed the evening of the same day.**

What price anarchy in the U.K.? The Sex Pistols might look ferocious, but so did heavy metal acts, and in any case the industry was used to marketing rebellion. What else was new? In fact the Sex Pistols would seriously disturb the status quo—at least for a time—by being the first rock act to turn their aggression against the industry itself, biting the hands that fed them.

And in this, as in other respects, it is almost impossible to interpret punk without considering it as a reaction against the hippy era that directly preceded it. As British writer Peter York put it in his book *Style Wars,* punk helped revive the generation gap:

**This wonderful market segmentation, first invented in the fifties, had been quiescent for seven years, during which, embarrassingly, young denim parents brought up in the Wonderworld of Teen themselves understood what their**

kids liked. The class element aside, the New Wave really represents a revolt of the young against the youngish.[10]

Style had never been so important to a rock movement. Indeed, when *Creem* first outlined the stirrings of the new age (not in London in 1976, but in New York in 1975), it was in Lisa Robinson's style column "Eleganza":

> **Patti Smith, Television, the Ramones, and perhaps the Talking Heads are evolving a totally new *look*, as well as a sound. There's a decidedly chiaroscuro (dictionary definition: arrangement of light and dark parts to create a pictorial vision) feel to these bands; a spare, stark, no-nonsense visual. So anti-fashion that it has become, for those of us looking closely, a fashion itself. . . . But more than an attempt to look conservative as an emotional backlash to a mob of flashy posers, there's an avant-garde nostalgia at work here as well as a desire to strip away all excess popstar trappings. . . . One comes away from these bands realizing more than ever that so many musicians—whose names I'd rather not mention—just look silly and old fashioned these days.[11]**

Punk style, in music and fashion, defined itself in opposition to the sloppiness of the late hippy era in the early seventies. It replaced all the floating nature wear and amorphous good will with an image that depended on monochrome, on hard edges, and a lot of symbolic violence. Late hippy fashion had been nostalgic and utopian, like the music itself, offering a melange of ethnic wear from American Indian to American farmworker to Eastern mystic, and although it was essentially costuming it reflected a certain naïve belief in the power of clothes to bestow the qualities of those civilizations—harmony, closeness to nature, spiritual enlightenment—on the wearer.

Punk had its own set of delusions about "you are what you

wear," leading to the spectacle of middle-class children dressing up in a fantasy of proletarian aggression and lying desperately about their backgrounds. (Joe Strummer was just one
of many punk musicians who had a private school education
to hide). However punk style, being a reaction against hippy
innocence, was never meant to be taken literally: it was always deliberately complex and hard to read.

With punk, the clothes came before the music. It was certainly the first rock movement to start in a boutique. As Malcolm McLaren, the Sex Pistols' manager, says, "I was just a
haberdasher, selling the odd whip or chain . . ."[12] when he
decided to manage some of the young delinquents who hung
around his King's Road clothes store and who had stolen
enough PA equipment to be able to form a band.

McLaren (ex-art student, ex-manager of the New York
Dolls) had started the store with Vivienne Westwood (a fashion designer of genius) in the mid-seventies under the name
Let It Rock. Fervent believers in the revolutionary potential of
youth and style, they began selling fifties revival clothes in a
doomed attempt to awaken the radical energy in the old
British teddy boy cults, until they were forced to acknowledge
defeat. They rechristened the shop Too Fast to Live, Too Young
to Die and began selling fifties biker gear, but it wasn't until
they moved into fetishist clothing and renamed the store Sex
that they found the key: perversion was the last taboo, a
guaranteed source of outrage and disruption. By combining
fetishist images with youthful rebellion McLaren and Westwood found the way to send shock waves through Britain.

Punk style, as first defined by Westwood, was a collage of
references, and in keeping with the new reaction against
hippy naïveté and sincerity, nothing meant what it seemed to
say: the fashion for fetishist clothing had nothing to do with
sex, early punks' habit of wearing swastikas nothing to do
with neofascism. The clothes sold at Sex were expensive, but
there was a do-it-yourself quality inherent in Westwood's love
of the trashy, the ugly, the ripped, and discarded. her style

lent itself to being homemade. Out of it developed an extraordinarily sophisticated street style that offered a spontaneous demonstration of postmodernism by people who had never even heard of the word. In Dick Hebdige's words in *Subculture:*

> **Punk reproduced the entire sartorial history of postwar working class youth in "cut up" form, combining elements which had originally belonged to completely different epochs. There was a chaos of quiffs and leather jackets, brothel creepers and winkle pickers, plimsolls and paka macs, moddy crops and skinhead strides, drainpipes and vivid socks, bum freezers and bovver boots—all kept "in place" and "out of time" by the spectacular adhesives: the safety pins and plastic clothes pegs, the bondage straps and bits of string which attracted so much horrified and fascinated attention.[13]**

But if the style came first, the style in itself was not enough. As McLaren said in 1987 in *i-D* magazine:

> **Music was always important to those clothes. . . . If people don't get a sense of emergency from the music they're not going to be interested. You've got to have attitude or else it won't work. To be honest with you, at the time the group was only a means to sell more clothes —the only reason I got involved with the Sex Pistols was to sell more trousers. It worked, but in the end the clothes weren't so important.[14]**

It had to be style plus music plus attitude. Initially, of course, it was the attitude that attracted attention. The Sex Pistols' first major entry into national British consciousness came on October 23, 1976, when they and some punk fans appeared on an early evening television program for an interview with Bill Grundy. There was drinking in the hospitality lounge before the show, which was live; on air Grundy taunted the group, asking them to be outrageous. They laughed and swore and said "fuck" a few times on family-hour TV, and the next day the press erupted in a frenzy: "TV Fury at Rock Cult Filth."

Afterwards, the group refused to apologize. This was one of the first signs that their attitude was for real, and that when they talked about being "honest" they meant they would not play the public relations game. EMI had begun to realize this group was genuinely antisocial, both in terms of bad behavior and in the sense of being opposed to the established order of things. In the meantime, punk was being diagnosed publicly not as a new music style but as a social problem. The Grundy show coincided with the first mass-media investigation of punk meaning in a *Daily Mirror* spread that tried to decipher the fans' motivation—punk was treated as a bizarre cult—by determining the symbolism of the ripped clothes and safety pins.

On December 7, 1976, the chairman of EMI gave an address at the company's annual general meeting which included these comments on the Sex Pistols scandal:

**Sex Pistols is a pop group devoted to a new form of music known as "punk rock." It was contracted for recording purposes by EMI Records Limited in October 1976—an unknown group offering some promise, in the view of our recording executives, like many other pop groups of different kinds that we have signed. In this context it must be remembered that the recording industry has signed many pop groups, initially controversial, who have in the fullness of time become wholly acceptable and contributed to the development of modern music. . . . I need hardly add that we shall do everything we can to restrain [the Sex Pistols'] public behavior, although this is a matter over which we have no real control.[15]**

The press coverage fueled public outrage, which inspired more press coverage, and once this roller coaster started running it was out of anyone's control—including that of EMI or

Malcolm McLaren. The TV scandal was followed by the launch of the White Riot tour with the Clash and the Damned, which drew so many public protests that most of the dates had to be canceled. On January 4, 1977, the British press reported that the Sex Pistols had thrown up in an airport lounge on their way to Europe, an event that created such fascination that the story went out over the international wire services and was reproduced in small newspapers all over the United States. The Pistols had become modern folk devils almost overnight; on January 6, 1977, they were sacked from EMI.

By far the best contemporary account of this saga is *The Sex Pistols* by Fred and Judy Vermorel, who gathered interviews and documents on the spot. They interviewed Leslie Hill, the managing director of EMI, who explained why the company couldn't continue working with the group:

**Now supposing we'd done what we usually do with them on tour, which is to have a press party or a party at the end of the do, or some sort of reception. There would have been a riot . . . there would have been people outside protesting, there would have been photographers everywhere, there would have been press people everywhere. It's not an environment in which we can operate in a normal fashion.**[16]

How could EMI send out a press kit, Hill pointed out with some justice, when the only headlines shrieked outrage and disgust? The whole public relations machine, which the music industry had built up over decades to filter information to the press, wasn't geared to something like this: a group who didn't care about being liked. Most disconcerting, for EMI, the group refused all requests to lie low until the bad publicity blew over and the company could help them "rebuild their career." It was this refusal to let their record company screen them from the public that marked the real break with the past. After all, the Pistols were hardly the first group to throw up in an airport or to turn up drunk at their record company's offices or to swear in public. The early seventies had seen far worse cases of rock 'n' roll excess in terms of drug taking, the abuse of fans, and the destruction of property. However, groups like Led Zeppelin wanted to keep their excesses private, and they saw no conflict of interest between themselves and their record company. The Sex Pistols did.

This opposition was fueled by McLaren's theories (developed in partnership with Vivienne Westwood and artist Jamie Reid) about cultural confrontation: crucial to his management of the Sex Pistols was his quite visionary understanding of the mass media, and how publicity could be used to anarchic effect. He had absorbed the lesson of the sixties—that the music industry was able to market and therefore neutralize any form of rock rebellion—and found a way of counteracting that process by turning the industry's publicity machine against itself. McLaren's original plan had been to create a manufactured group like the Monkees or the Bay City Rollers, except that this would be a "Bay City Rollers of Outrage." In other words, this group would be so vile, so wildly amateur, and so offensive that just by being successful they would make a mockery of the industry that sold them. (That the music was exciting turned out to be vital to the development of punk as a movement, but it was not part of the original plan.) If the "antigroup" became a teen sensation, like the Bay City Rollers, no record company would be able to resist them, and yet no record company could promote them without getting its fingers burnt. Selling such vileness would make a mockery of all the industry's public relations tricks, and yet, at the same time, it would genuinely disseminate a disruptive, rebellious influence to the kids. Even with hindsight (even with his own hindsight), it is difficult to know whether McLaren was operating on a chaotic series of intuitions or according to an orchestrated plan, but what is clear is that he was the first rock manager to use the subversive possibilities of hype.

A&M Records signed the Sex Pistols on March 9, 1977, and fired them a week later; evidently panicking at the continuing media outrage. The company was particularly alarmed about the reaction they would get to the next single "God Save the Queen" in the year of the Queen's Jubilee. Once more such cowardice worked to the group's profit, as the Pistols kept the £75,000 advance, having already earned £50,000 from being fired by EMI. Next they signed with Virgin, an independent company that had originally serviced the sixties counterculture and ended the 1970s as Britain's most successful example of hip capitalism. Virgin was a symbol of everything the Sex Pistols supposedly detested, but the relationship functioned for the rest of the group's brief life, not least because the Sex Pistols' hype worked entirely to Virgin's advantage—the company preserved its "countercultural" image while signing up a new generation of pop stars and quietly dropping its progressive and "avant-garde" pretensions.

The punk generation (which Virgin was now wooing) was not only highly aware of the pop industry, they were also highly critical of how it worked. This was as true of punk journalists as of the bands—the two new stars of the pop press, Julie Burchill and Tony Parsons, trumpeted their new purity against the older writers' corruption: they described themselves as "the only unbiased rock writers in the world—no trips to America, no free lunches, no payola, no nothing." But punk antagonism to the way the industry operated often took the form of mere style criticism, insulting record company executives (in their awful flared trousers and satin bomber jackets) for being old, fat, and unhip. This obsession with clothes was partly because punk was the "rebellion of the young against the youngish," partly because punk was pop music at its most self-referential. The original punk bands of 1976 and 1977 were obsessed with hatred for the stars of the previous generation, and used to slag off the Who or the Rolling Stones with extraordinary venom—with more venom indeed than they directed toward the government.

The Sex Pistols' wars with their record companies also set a fashion of hostility toward the major labels which was more than a matter of hippy rhetoric. The second punk generation, which emerged in the late seventies, was more likely to sign to one of the host of small independent labels that had sprung up to service the new music, sharing the musicians' style and attitude. "Independence" was often illusory—many small labels signed distribution deals that effectively made them into research and development outposts for the majors—but there was one positive effect: the industry was far more flexible and responsive in coping with the many new groups and styles that rose out of the fragmentation of punk than it had been in handling the fragmentation of sixties rock. In this respect, in its hostility to the established music business, punk actually helped regenerate the British industry at the moment when mainstream pop sales were collapsing.

Of course punk bands also turned their aggression on record companies because they had no other real political focus. The great irony of punk was that although it had a threatening and violent style, and a far more rigorous and uncompromising antibourgeois attitude than rock had shown in the sixties, it had no clear battles to fight—at least no battles it knew it could win. In that sense it reflected Britain's political apathy in the late seventies, with its corresponding retreat into the compensation of personal expression in private life. Punks might talk about the destruction of British society and anarchy in the U.K., but as a dream rather than a serious plan. As Siouxsie of the Banshees said in 1976 to Mark Perry, the editor of *Sniffin' Glue:* "We may not have anarchy in the streets, but at least we can have it in our little club." [17]

Punk's apocalyptic style—torn clothes, white shell-shocked faces, zombie makeup—was a fragmented reflection of society's fears in the late seventies, absorbing anxiety about nuclear war, recession, unemployment, and social breakdown, and throwing it out again in this nightmare style. But it was a largely symbolic aggression, and it worked on a symbolic level: the Sex Pistols' most controversial song attacked a symbol, a living color postcard, the Queen. The second generation of punk bands, less anarchic and more orthodoxly left-wing than the first, organized specific campaigns like Rock Against Racism, but there was never a sense, as there had been in the sixties, that rock was articulating a mass consciousness for social change, nor was there a single burning issue, as Vietnam had been for the sixties, to give it a sense of purpose.

So what did punk actually do, apart from reviving the British pop industry? At its best and most extreme expression, in the Sex Pistols, punk worked as a series of brilliant gestures, confrontations that caused havoc as long as the ideas were still in flux, when no one knew what exactly this was or how to handle it. But when the dust died down and the panic was over, all that was left was rock 'n' roll. Johnny Rotten commented:

**I think you've got to be an idiot to think that any of that meant anything. It changes nothing. It does not make you a better person just because you've got a Pistols album. It doesn't lower your fucking rent. It does nothing. It's escapism. All music is.**[18]

What else did we expect? How could anyone have expected consistent politics and effective social change from a culture based on teenagers? The teenager's whole dynamic is based on fashion: on peer group pressure and imitation, on the endless search for novelty, sensation, and change. Punk's weakness was to treat clothes and haircuts as revolutionary acts. In 1976 the punk fanzine *Sniffin' Glue* asked the Clash whether style was that important and they replied, "Like trousers, like brain," as if it was that easy to get a new brain.

In this suggestion Joe Strummer oddly echoed David Crosby, and looking back it seems clear that the punk and hippy eras were much closer to each other than to what came before or after. Both believed absolutely in the importance of

rock, in the virtue of rebellion, and in authenticity and commitment. And when punk switched from anarchy and may-
hem to orthodox left-wing politics, it adopted the same
notions of grass-roots networks and alternative distribution
systems (often run by former hippies), that had been so important in the sixties counterculture. The two movements even
operated out of the same urban areas. In London punk took
over the old hippy hangouts of Notting Hill Gate and the
King's Road; in New York punk clothing and record stores
sprang up on the Lower East Side next to health food shops
and boutiques, painted with faded sunflowers, selling their
last stocks of hashpipes and patchouli oil. It was precisely
because they believed in the same things that punks were so
antagonistic to hippies: in many ways it was a family quarrel.

But if punk was the hostile child of the hippy movement, it
had broken with the past by wedding pop and rock hype
together. From pop it got its conscious exploitation of the
media, from rock its stance as the rebellious outsider, and the
marriage enabled punk—briefly—to exploit hype while
challenging it on its own ground, both through its consistent
attack on the values of the music industry and by exposing to
its audience how that industry worked. However, this self-
consciousness proved extremely diffficult to sustain for those
post-punk bands of the late seventies who were left to carry
the torch.

The shining heroes of British rock in 1978 were the Gang
of Four, a group who had formed at Leeds University and
were making front covers of the music press before they grad-
uated. Thanks to a slashing guitar sound, fiercely energetic
live shows, and clever lyrics, they were able to fill the gap left
by the demise of first-generation punk, while their love of
theorizing (a legacy from student days) made them perfect
heroes for the increasingly earnest music press. They were
inaccurately labeled Marxists (their politics were undergrad-
uate and hazy), and for a time, the Gang of Four seemed the
answer to the punk audience's search for purity and rigor.

The pressure became intolerable, as the group's every career move was expected to conform to the highest ideals. They had begun on the kind of small independent label that was then a symbol of rock ideological purity. As the big offers came, the group spent months debating whether they should stay in the independent ghetto, which still meant restricted sales and distribution, or enter the mainstream by signing with a major label. Steeped in punk and art school theories about radical intervention in popular culture, they chose the mainstream option and signed with EMI; the justification they gave was the same as that used in the sixties—only a big company could really help them get their message across. Submerged under this lay an even more traditional element of rock 'n' roll: desire, the quality that made them a classic rock group in the first place. Why shouldn't they have huge audiences? Why shouldn't they have the excitement of major success? Why shouldn't they—hard as it was to admit—make money?

For all their naïveté, the Gang of Four did try and face the contradictions of a politically committed rock band trying to make it inside the capitalist system—but eventually those contradictions destroyed them. Under attack from fans and the music press for "selling out" (another sixties notion) to the mainstream, the group was uncooperative with their record company and uncertain as to how to maintain their integrity while marketing themselves. When their first single on EMI began to sell, they were offered a spot on Britain's most successful music show, *Top of the Pops*, which would virtually guarantee them a place in the charts. But *Top of the Pops* demanded they change one line in the song, a reference to condoms. Uneasy about commercialism, and feeling the need to make a stand somewhere, they refused to change the line, and the appearance was canceled. The song was not a hit. Once that moment had passed—and catching the moment means everything in popular music—their career began to decline, they fell prey to internal arguments and uncertainty, and the best group of 1978 never fulfilled their potential.

Too much puritanism was obviously bad for music, and post-punk austerity was beginning to pall. From now on the movement split into a multitude of styles that can be divided roughly into rock and pop—for in spite of the upheavals of punk, music was still being made in those competing terms. On one side were the punk loyalists, who operated on the independent labels, and who clung to the clothes, the sound, and what they saw as the ideals of 1976. In retreat from the present and lacking the insouciance of the original punks, they evolved into a brand of neo-hippies (often with vegetarian, pacifist, and mystic ideals) and pursued a determinedly noncommercial (either abrasive or dirgelike) musical course. They joined the ranks of other die-hard rock conservatives, like the fifties' teds and the sixties' hippies; but meanwhile, in the main arena, a shiny new pop era began to take the floor.

## CAREER OPPORTUNITIES

The most startling renegade punk career was Adam Ant's. Overnight it seemed (if with a little advice from Malcolm McLaren) he went from moody punk cult figure on London's indie bohemian scene to teenybop idol, dancing around on *Top of the Pops* with ribbons in his hair (and a CBS contract in his pocket). His career moves were followed closely by his old friends.

How could the same generation who had made punk make commercial pop and still feel good about themselves? The answer lies in David Bowie and the tradition he created of pop as performance art. In the early seventies Bowie was a teen idol who combined the flounce and swagger and androgyny of glam rock with a strategy. He became a superstar through the sci-fi persona of Ziggy Stardust in which he acted out the fantasy of the rock star as tormented superhero, thus endowing his real self with an aura of power and mystery. Bowie followed this with a chameleonlike series of changes of fashion and musical style which actually mirrored the pop process itself: its fickleness and restlessness, its obsession with surfaces and images, with glamor and unreality. By embodying this process within himself (and demonstrating an almost magical ability to stay in fashion through the seventies) Bowie presented himself as the master puppeteer, the magician who had understood the secret of eternal pop success. His control of his own stardom was the validation for everything he did; Bowie's message was that a pop star was not a passive commodity but an auteur, whose creative field was the marketplace itself.

David Bowie was a graduate of another important influence on British pop music: art school, a traditional escape route for bright working-class kids, and a breeding ground for young bands from the Beatles on. (Even the Sex Pistols played their first gig at Saint Martin's School of Art, and the punk movement probably had more art students than proletarians). British art schools usually include fashion departments, and provide not just a visual education but an atmosphere in which bizarre dressing is encouraged; this kind of do-it-yourself avant-garde fashion has filtered through into British youth culture, where self-expression is seen in terms of outrageous style.

Art means very different things to pop and rock. In rock it means a search for something profound and lasting, to make the popular song function in the way that great art does. It is a search that has given us Bob Dylan and the Velvet Underground on the one hand, and many ghastly rock operas and concept albums on the other. In pop, art is much more concerned with style and gesture (Roxy Music are the archetypal art pop band) and with the ironic use of pop history by switching between different eras and genres. Pop was postmodernist before the term was invented.

On a street level the pop stress on style and attitude elevated posing into an art form. And in the early eighties, the most flamboyant poseur on the London club scene was Boy George O'Dowd. He used to enter pubs filled with skinheads dressed as a nun; when he signed to Virgin Records it seemed the final proof that dressing up was enough to make a career. (It turned out to be a bonus that he could sing.) In the mid-eighties, the introduction of MTV combined with the enervation of American pop to make Boy George into one of pop's most unlikely superstars. In Britain he retained a disturbing quality, redolent of London nightlife, transvestism, and the gay art and fashion world; in America, where he reached audiences through a series of playful videos, George was seen as a kind of benign extraterrestrial, a pop E.T.

More conventional British stars had already broken through MTV—like Duran Duran, pretty boys whose videos presented a vivid fantasy of sunshine sex and exotic locations. The British groups' understanding of style and presentation was enough to launch a new "British Invasion"—at least until a new generation of American acts like Cyndi Lauper and Madonna proved that they could use the same tricks. Video had transformed the music business, and it drew all performers, whether pop or rock, into a new and powerful process of image creation.

Before considering the ways in which video has changed the face of hype, we should return to the question of what pop and rock really mean. As both encompass many musical styles, it is easier to assess them in terms of the values they represent.

Pop stands for mutability and glitter. Its mode is the 45 single and the pinup, and its value is measured by record sales and the charts. Pop is about dreams and escapism and ecstatic moments; it believes in clichés and its philosophy is "give the people what they want." It is egalitarian by nature —anyone can make it—and capitalist.

Rock is about the search for permanence within the free-floating values of the marketplace. It is about tradition (blues, country, and folk roots), and it is hierarchical in that it believes in geniuses and heroes. Its mode is the long-playing album and the in-depth interview. Rock wants deep emotion and catharsis and truth; it has a religious element that pop does not. Rock believes in originality and self-expression in defiance of crass commercialism.

If this seems to suggest that pop means shallow and rock means depth, consider which is the more profound experience —Smoky Robinson's "The Tracks of My Tears" or Led Zeppelin's "Stairway to Heaven"? And yet the one is a pop, the other a rock classic. And far from being rigid categories, pop and rock often intertwine—where would you put "River Deep Mountain High"? Where would you put Prince? How do you classify punk?

To take the most successful examples from each category, rock in the 1980s is exemplified by Bruce Springsteen, pop by Madonna. Springsteen, dressed in worker's denim, eschewing glamor, proclaiming his loyalty and affection for his lower-middle class New Jersey roots, is a byword for authenticity. His songs deal with humble lives and his music is a synthesis of the great traditions of the past, in rock 'n' roll, rhythm and blues, and country ballads. He rarely gives interviews and seems appalled by hype. Madonna, of course, embraces hype like an old-fashioned Hollywood starlet (her obvious role model) and has had a success that is due as much to her "bad girl" style, her use of the press, and—above all—her videos, as it is to her music.

But rather than stressing the obvious differences between Bruce Springsteen and Madonna, let's see what they have in common. The most obvious shared quality is their striving. Both are known to work out, both present their live shows as heavy athletic achievements. Behind this lies the old show business ethic of giving the audience their money's worth, and being seen to do so. Madonna's manager ex- lained on an early tour that she would play medium-sized venues, not stadiums, because he wanted the audience to see her sweat.

But the striving wouldn't mean much if the performers weren't also seen to be making it. Neither failure nor the hippy indifference to the work ethic are popular in the eighties. Both Madonna and Springsteen represented success—working hard for it, then finding it—and holding out the promise, through their example, that you can get it too. And they offer something of a formula for how to get it: Madonna's vegetarianism and strict athletic regime, Springsteen's refusal to take drugs and indifference to alcohol. You can make it if you try. This gives their material a paradoxical quality when either one sings about failure. When Madonna sings about heartbreak and vulnerability in love, she still holds before us the image of the sex symbol, the tough ambitious girl who clawed her way to the top. Springsteen sings about the poor and defeated in triumphant, soaring rock 'n' roll songs that also hold before us the image of his own success. A crucial factor here is the way video has changed the public response to a song—it holds the artists' image in mind while you listen, so that the image and the song's message become confused and intertwined.

No pop artist can be successful *at the wrong time*, or by running totally counter to the popular mood, and the eighties mood was in favor of guilt-free, well-earned success. Springsteen, with his concern for the working man, his classic liberal values, his evocation of Woody Guthrie et al., would seem in absolute opposition to the spirit of the Reagan age. But what an artist *says* and what he is actually *projecting* can be very different things. A classic example is the use of the American flag on *Born in the U.S.A.* as the backdrop to a close-up of Springsteen's ass, clad in torn jeans, with an old baseball cap hanging out of one pocket. As Springsteen himself explained to Kurt Loden in *Rolling Stone:* "I didn't have any secret message. I don't do that very much. We had the flag on the cover because the first song was called 'Born in the U.S.A.,' and the theme of the record kind of follows from the themes I've been writing about for the last six or seven years. But the flag is a powerful image, and when you set that stuff loose, you don't know what's gonna be done with it."[19]

There is no need to call this cynicism or calculation. Springsteen has always been temperamentally conservative (his music is steeped in the past) although politically liberal, and he is the most consciously American artist of recent years. But that contradiction allowed him to sing songs of liberal social protest, and yet be the most popular mainstream rock 'n' roll artist of a deeply reactionary age. Dave Marsh, in *Glory Days*, castigates CBS correspondent Bernard Goldberg for declaring:

> **Bruce Springsteen sings about Americans—blue-collar Americans trapped and suffocating in old broken-down small towns. His songs are about working-class people, desperate people hanging on to the American dream by a thread. . . . He touches his fans and they touch him. His shows are like old-time revivals with the same old-time message: If they work hard enough and long enough, like Springsteen himself, they can also make it to the promised land.**[20]

Goldberg may have misunderstood Springsteen's lyrics, but not his total effect, in which compassion for the defeated means less than his own blinding success. Public perception has always been impossible to measure but what is clear is that now, more than ever before, rock stars have no control over how their images are received. The video onslaught and the general electronic surfeit of images have made it very unlikely that one single message will get through. The September 25, 1986, issue of *Rolling Stone*, the special college issue, had an article devoted to "The Baby Bankers," the new breed of yuppie graduates making fortunes on Wall Street. One of the typical cases they picked on was a chillingly bright-eyed and eager 23-year-old named Harry Nudelman.

Harry had a job in mergers-and-acquisitions, proclaimed oil raider T. Boone Pickens to be his personal hero, and had two photographs taped above his desk at work: his parents, and Bruce Springsteen.

For a performer, control over the meaning of what he does has always meant having control over his image, over how his audience will perceive him. This has always been true, but never more so than since the new cynicism about marketing introduced by punk, and the fusion between hit songs and visual images introduced by video. For a performer like Springsteen the more he tries to detach his image from that sales process, the more artificial his image becomes—if only because the maintenance of his integrity requires a continual watchfulness and involvement in overseeing his own marketing process. It is as self-conscious as his decision—as a multimillionaire rock star—to always appear publicly in humble working man's clothes. Madonna, with her unabashed artificiality and calculation is actually presenting a more genuine image of herself and her position than Springsteen, and finds her image easier to control.

But of course no performer can actually control how an audience receives them or their work, and one of the greatest dilemmas for all pop artists (and those with a financial stake in their success) is how to ensure the longevity of their career. The problem lies in the volatility of the pop-rock market, and the answer is to build a personal identification and loyalty that can transcend it. At its most intense a rock star can become, like the greatest movie stars, one of the saints of the electronic age: an icon to be worshiped for themselves rather than for anything they have actually done. The pursuit of the highest level of modern celebrity means developing a persona that can attract this kind of intense personal identification and fascination. This is not the same as selling records: Phil Collins, the most faceless of modern pop stars, regularly goes platinum even though most of his audience probably don't know one personal detail about him—and could care less. No one worships Phil Collins; they have simply made him very rich.

The most obvious pursuit of pop celebrity in recent years has been led by Madonna, who made that pursuit a conscious part of her own image. Through Madonna, we vicariously realize all our own ambitions toward the magic of Hollywood and celebrityhood. From the beginning she consciously placed herself in the tradition of glamorous blondes, and there could have been no greater proof of Madonna's arrival in the contemporary hall of fame than when she was featured on the cover of The National Enquirer (August 26, 1986) with a headline that read "Madonna's Bizarre Belief—She Says Marilyn Monroe Is Reincarnated in Her." Inside we learned that Madonna had converted a room in her house into a Marilyn Monroe shrine, and a "friend" reported: "Several parallels have convinced Madonna that she is Marilyn reincarnated. They stem back to her childhood . . . she feels driven to relive the Marilyn Monroe story—only with a happy ending. She's determined not to be a victim of circumstances this time." Added the insider, "Madonna feels she is destined to finish what she started as Marilyn. She told me, 'Marilyn and I are at the top again. But this time we are going to stay there!' "

Madonna is a supreme example of self-invention—that is what her entire public persona is based on—and she was clearly on to a good thing in the cross between old-style Hollywood and eighties health-consciousness and ambition. However, the emphasis was different at the beginning of her career. Like any good self-inventer, she has adjusted her persona to fit the times and presented each new account of herself with total conviction. So in the early eighties, when Prince was making his first waves and *Thriller* reigned supreme, Madonna presented herself as the streetwise Catholic girl from Detroit, who grew up equally at home with black and white music. There was nothing false in any of this; it's just that Madonna emphasizes what she needs to according to circumstance.

The story of the Madonna persona can be told through her videos. In "Borderline" we see her in sleeveless denim jacket and sweatpants, like a hip little gang member, dancing in an urban wasteland with tough attractive Hispanic boys. These streetlife scenes are intercut with a black and white sequence —not fantasy but another aspect of Madonna's reality—as a chic fashion photographer picks her up in a white sports car and takes her to his studio for a session in which she metamorphoses into glamorous magazine images. We have here a personal drama, the story of Madonna the romantic, Madonna the tease, torn between her different lovers. This is counterpointed by the song, which offers a reversal of the video narration: Madonna is singing about a boy who confuses her, drives her wild with uncertainty, but in the video— which is what we really believe—we know that it is Madonna who drives boys crazy. What we also get from this is an enormous sense of potential: that this is a girl who could be a star. Already, at the very beginning of Madonna's video life, we have become emotionally involved with her ambition.

Madonna may well have been the first singer to understand how to make videos work within the pop career, and how to use them in the development of a persona. A pop career depends on a sequence of new releases, each record offering a further chapter in achievement, each one building on the last. Madonna's great secret—and she always has had a great deal of input into her videos—was to realize that although videos can function as minimovies, they must function sequentially, and relate back to each other, to provide a continuing sense of the artist's life.

The next video, 1984's "Lucky Star" forsook narrative for a tight focus on image: Madonna in sunglasses, blacklace gloves, giving a seductive, cheeky wink at the camera. This was video technique at its simplest and most effective: wiggle and look straight into the lens. It established Madonna both as a fashion symbol (crossing punk style with black street fashion, aerobics, and a dance student's artiness) and as the crossover girl: when the camera pulled back we saw that she was dancing with two boys, one black, one white.

Men play the shadowy glamor role in Madonna videos that women usually play to male stars. In "Like a Virgin" (also released in 1984) the video and the song that made her a major star, the lover is a darkly romantic figure with a GQ profile, who is seen only in glimpses: Madonna is always the center of the camera's attention. "Like a Virgin" returned to the Madonna narrative, opening in archetypal fashion with a huge moon shining over Manhattan—the citadel of Madonna's early ambitions—as she draws up to a pier across from the city, dressed in track clothes, and gives a longing look before disappearing into the darkness. At the next cut we see her in a gondola in Venice, looking thinner and more glamorous than in previous video appearances, and showing us that Madonna has gone international. We see her then trailing through an empty palazzo in a baroque white wedding dress, courted by a mysterious, princely figure in a lion's mask. Not only is this "Beauty and the Beast" (videos like to throw in as many archetypes as possible), it evokes the image of the American girl who takes Europe by storm and marries an aristocrat. Beneath the surface message—a remarkably tasteless but effective lyric about how the right man can wipe all your sins away, sung to her most compulsive dance beat ever—what we are really being told is that Madonna has moved on to the world stage and is doing very well.

All this is confirmed in 1985's "Material Girl," also directed by Mary Lambert. One of Madonna's great gifts, and a key to her stardom, is that she is never afraid to state the obvious: subtler talents have hesitated in the wings while Madonna, with her magnificent energy, grabbed the prize. "Material Girl" hammers the message home; it also suggests that Madonna had begun to think it was time to find a way to build a more adult and stable career in films. It begins with a producer and his assistant watching a screening of the very video we are about to see, as the producer says, "She's fantastic, I knew she could be a star." Being a Madonna video, it leavens the obvious with a touch of humor: this little vignette is also presented as a parody of Hollywood. We are then drawn into the video itself, a straight homage (a nice way of saying imitation) to Marilyn Monroe singing "Diamonds Are a Girl's Best Friend" in pink satin on a Hollywood staircase; this is intercut with another Madonna love story, designed to show the girl is soft-centered at heart. The song proved invaluable for headlines—Madonna had given herself a title, "The Material Girl"—and the video was praised for its stylishness. However, it could also be seen as the beginning of Madonna's decline as an interesting person. She had always been so modern, so daring; even if you didn't warm to her she seemed to know about places and styles you didn't. Now she was offering nostalgia and conventional movie imagery.

"Into the Groove" was a throwback to the earlier Madonna persona, because this was from the soundtrack to *Desperately Seeking Susan,* the Susan Seidelman movie that turned the Madonna of the "Borderline" video into a full-length movie character. Seidelman, the only film director who has understood how to use Madonna, realized that she was not an actress, but a fascinating personality and image: all Madonna had to do was to play a character very much like herself, but without direction and ambition. The movie was a huge hit; thanks partly to Madonna's name (she had just had her first worldwide hits), but the benefit was mutual. *Desperately Seeking Susan* established Madonna as a larger-than-life personality, a living fictional character, paving the way for her ascension into the first rank of celebrityhood, those few fit for the cover of the *National Enquirer,* the elite who are known only by their first names—Liz, Diana, Joan—and whose lives are so interesting they no longer have to do anything except *be.*

The next installment, "Angel," rapturously acknowledged this success. It begins with the sound of Madonna laughing and tumbles through a collage of scenes from all her past videos—and by implication, Madonna's own past—to show us how far she has come and where she has been. Her personal and video life were now becoming genuinely intertwined. Her romance and marriage to Sean Penn became part of the video narration when she released "Live to Tell," the theme song from Penn's movie *At Close Range,* with a video that cut soulful shots of Madonna singing a ballad (i.e., Madonna grows up) with scenes from her husband's movie.

The variety has continued. "Papa Don't Preach" went for early sixties style social realism, with a story of an unwed mother that drew blatantly on Madonna's much publicized early life and the tension between her and her strict Italian father to make an effective little soap opera. "True Blue" was straight sixties Spector-style nostalgia of a pretty banal kind, but this was followed by her best, and certainly most experimental video, "Open Your Heart." This begins in a stylized strip club, in which Madonna is displayed as an exploited, but untouchable sex object, safe behind glass as middle-aged men leer and drool, and ends in a burst for freedom as Madonna and a little boy do a Chaplinesque dance down some yellow brick road to safety and happiness. The message is that our girl may sell sexuality, but she is free.

It has been a triumphant video career, contrasting with her catastrophic attempts to be a real life actress in the films *Shanghai Surprise* and *Who's That Girl* in which Madonna tried, with painful ineptitude, to evoke the images of Jean Harlow, Carole Lombard, Marilyn Monroe, and Judy Holliday. (In the classic days of Hollywood, of course, Madonna wouldn't have had to try to act; she could just have continued to be herself.) Her invulnerability, that image of driving success that all her fans and imitators could identify with and vicariously share in, has been tarnished somewhat, although her recording success had never been affected by the movie flops.

But how Madonna survives into the nineties remains to be seen. Pop stars have, since the beginning, desperately sought a stability outside the youth market, usually in film. It's a hard and painful business, selling yourself, and any performer is faced with a constantly diminishing capital in the form of their own youth and attractiveness.

# BUGALU!

**B**oth Madonna and Bruce Springsteen are inextricably involved with hype. And hype will always be a highly-charged issue in pop and rock because it raises the question of the music's value: is this value intrinsic or is it determined purely by the marketplace? If it does have an intrinsic value (the rock belief) then hype is the market's attempt to distort our perceptions for commercial gain—to manipulate the public's responses, persuading them to accept what is flashy and meretricious rather than what is serious and good. However, if you think the value of the music is determined by what people get from it (the pop belief)—i.e., it is entirely subjective and only as valuable as the audience feels it to be—then hype is simply part of what one enjoys in pop. If it sells it's good; if not, not.

Much of the tension and excitement in popular music comes from the way it shifts between these two modes, so that the question of truth and significance and lasting value is always up for grabs. Remember that every new era in postwar popular music, from Sinatra to Elvis to the Sex Pistols to Prince has been dismissed as "hype." Each new generation claims its own music while their elders despair over their "manipulation": I'm not just talking about parents and children but about Grateful Dead fans dismissing the Sex Pistols as a pop hype, Sex Pistols fans dismissing Culture Club as shallow and meaningless, and so on.

These conflicts over authenticity are probably inevitable in a mass market cultural form that at times also fills the function of traditional high art, a form so varied that it is used by some as simple entertainment and others as something close to religion. And yet even at its most serious, some of our pleasure in popular music is always tied to its commercial processes. Why? Because popular music is more than just a sound. It is also a picture on a wall, an album cover, an interview, a fashion, a stadium concert shared with thousands, an adolescent's lonely fantasy. This imaginative dimension, like the music, is something that is bought and sold, but does that deny its meaning?

Which brings us back to "bugalu." Because here, at least, we find stability and assurance in the midst of pop/rock's wildly spinning values. Surely this is an absolutely worthless concept, something so risible—at once fatuously naive and crassly exploitative—that no one could have been taken in? After all it failed. But what if it hadn't? After all, who would have predicted the marketing of hippy culture? Or that British teenagers would start a fashion for safety pins through their noses? Or that American teenagers in the eighties would go for a Monkees revival tour? Lose sight of the improbable, and you lose sight of pop music itself. The point being, if bugalu had worked, it *would* now be important simply because it had meant something to the people who took part. Rather than a simple piece of corporate idiocy, it would have a new aura, one of nostalgia and affection. And they'd be marketing a bugalu revival right now.

**TOP 40 RADIO:** A fragment of the imagination

1. "The Storz Bombshell," *Television Magazine,* May 1957.
2. Brad Burkhardt, "Listener Myths and Realities," *Radio & Records,* January 23, 1987.
3. Ken Barnes, "Democratic Radio," in Marsh, ed., *The First Rock & Roll Confidential Report* (New York: Pantheon, 1985), pp. 44–45.
4. Radio Advertising Bureau figures, January 1988.
5. *Radio & Records Ratings Report and Directory,* Fall 1987.

**AIN'T NO MOUNTAIN HIGH ENOUGH:**
The politics of crossover

1. Andy Van de Voorde, "Crossing Over: Are Black Superstars Killing Black Music?" Baltimore *City Paper,* December 12, 1986.
2. *Ibid.*
3. *Ibid.*
4. *Ibid.*
5. Peter Guralnick, *Sweet Soul Music: Rhythm and Blues and the Southern Dream of Freedom* (New York: Harper and Row, 1986).
6. Malcolm X, *The Autobiography of Malcolm X* (New York: Random House, 1964).
7. *Ibid.*
8. *Ibid*

9. Greil Marcus, *Mystery Train: Images of America in Rock & Roll Music* (New York: E. P. Dutton, 1976).
10. Charles Hamm, *Music in the New World* (New York: W. W. Norton, 1983).
11. Guralnick, *Sweet Soul Music*.
12. Leroi Jones, *Blues People* (New York: Morrow Quill, 1963).
13. Anthony Heilbut, *The Gospel Sound: Good News and Bad Times* (New York: Simon and Schuster, 1971; revised edition, New York: Limelight Editions, 1985).
14. Bill C. Malone, *Country Music USA* (Austin: University of Texas Press, 1968).
15. Terence Trent D'Arby, interview in Q, October, 1987.
16. Ralph Ellison, *Shadow and Act* (New York: Vintage, 1964).

**VIDEO POP:** Picking up the pieces

1. W. F. Haug, *Critique of Commodity Aesthetics* (Cambridge: Polity Press, 1984), pp. 35–6.
2. J. B. Bernstein and Martin Cunning, "Crash from Chaos," *Cut*, January 1986, p. 14.
3. Ted Fox, *In the Groove* (New York: St. Martin's, 1986), p. 322.
4. Stephen Holden, "Musical Odyssey," *New York Times*, December 9, 1987.
5. *Ibid.*
6. *Ibid.*
7. *Guardian*, May 30, 1986.
8. Leslie Savan, "Rock Rolls Over," *Village Voice*, August 11, 1987, pp. 71–72.
9. Harry Ritchie, "A Larger Than Life Campaign," *Glasgow Herald*, August 12, 1987.
10. Savan, *Rock Rolls Over*.
11. Dave Marsh, *Glory Days* (New York: Pantheon, 1987), p. 361.
12. Fox, *In the Groove*, p. 324.
13. Michael Goldberg, "The Wisdom of Solomon," *Rolling Stone*, November 22, 1984, p. 85.
14. John Ryan and Richard A. Peterson, "The Product Image," in J. S. Ettema and D. Charles (eds.), *Individuals in Mass Media Organizations: Creativity and Constraints* (Beverly Hills: Sage, 1982).

**15.** Heikki Hellman, "The New State of Competition in the Record Industry," *Sociologia* 20 (4):355.
**16.** Mark Cooper, "Tapes That Time Forgot," Q, May 1987, pp. 16–18.
**17.** Geoff Travis, "Speakers Corner," *Catalogue*, March 1987, p. 27.
**18.** Fox, *In the Groove*, p. 291.
**19.** Will Straw, "The Contexts of Music Video: Popular Music and Postmodernism in the 1980s," *Working Papers in Communication* (Montreal: McGill University, 1987).
**20.** Fox, *In the Groove*, p. 315.
**21.** Gillian Davies, "New Technology, Music Production, and Copyright," *IFPI Review 1986*, p. 27.
**22.** Goldberg, "The Wisdom," p. 87.
**23.** *Ibid.*
**24.** Davies, "New Technology," p. 31.
**25.** Fox, *In the Groove*, pp. 334–36.
**26.** Chris Cutler, "Skill: The Negative Case for Some New Music Technology," *Re Records Quarterly* (3), 1986.
**27.** Robert Christgau, "Down by Law," *Village Voice*, March 25, 1986.
**28.** "Thorn Goes for Yuppie Market," *Guardian*, December 11, 1986.
**29.** Torin Douglas, "Magazines That Could Explode the Media Myth," *Observer*, April 28, 1987.

**THE ENEMY WITHIN:** Sex, rock, and identity

**1.** Jonathan Dollimore, "Homophobia and Sexual Difference," *Oxford Literary Review* 8, 1986.
**2.** Rodney Garland, *The Heart of Exile* (London: W. H. Allen, 1953).
**3.** Dwight MacDonald, "A Caste, A Culture, A Market," *The New Yorker*, November 22 and 29, 1958.
**4.** Richard Wightman Fox and T. J. Jackson Lears (eds.), *The Culture of Consumption* (New York: Pantheon, 1983).
**5.** Christopher Booker, *The Neophiliacs* (London: Collins, 1969).
**6.** MacDonald, "A Caste."

7. For a fuller account of the predominately white, college-based youth culture of the twenties, see Paula Fass, *The Damned and the Beautiful* (New York: Oxford University Press, 1977).
8. J. D. Salinger, *The Catcher in the Rye* (Boston: Little, Brown, 1945).
9. Charles White, *The Life and Times of Little Richard* (London: Pan, 1984), p. 63.
10. For an account of postwar black music and its milieu, see Ted Fox, *Showtime at the Apollo* (New York: Holt, Rinehart, and Winston, 1983).
11. "Presliad," in Greil Marcus, *Mystery Train* (New York: E. P. Dutton, 1977), gives an acute analysis of the many musical, social, and cultural factors behind Elvis's music and myth. See also the liner notes by Peter Guralnick to the 1987 reissue (RCA, UK) of *The Sun Sessions*.
12. MacDonald, "A Caste."
13. The title of a chapter by Frank Owen in *The Teen Age Book*, Ann Seymour, ed. (London: Sampson Low, 1950).
14. Abigail Van Buren, *Dear Teenager* (New York: Random House, 1959).
15. *The New Musical Express 1956 Annual*, p. 95.
16. David Dalton and Ron Cayen, *James Dean: An American Icon* (New York: St. Martin's, 1984) offers a good explanation of Dean's enduring power.
17. Andy Medhurst, "Can Chaps Be Pin-Ups," *Ten-8* (17) 1985.
18. Dollimore, "Homophobia."
19. MacDonald, "A Caste."
20. Peter Biskind, *Seeing Is Believing* (New York: Pantheon, 1983).
21. George Orwell, "Raffles and Miss Blandish," October 1944.
22. "Spiv" is a peculiarity of English slang, the pejorative reversal of a word, like "yobs" ("boy" backwards)."Spiv" reversed the wartime VIP (Very Important Person) to describe a black marketeer, who was more important to the population at large.
23. Geoffrey Pearson, *Hooligan: A History of Respectable Fears* (London: MacMillan Press, 1983) contains much detail on pre-teenage youth gangs and the moral panics they aroused.
24. This youth group inspired the lost juvenile delinquency film classic, *Cosh Boy* (U.K., 1952) and several novels, like Bruce

Walker, *Cosh Boy: The Graphic Story of London's Juvenile Jungle* (London: Ace Paperbacks, 1959).

**25.** Booker, *Neophiliacs.*

**26.** Medhurst, "Can Chaps Be Pin Ups."

**27.** Jon Savage, "Teds," *The Face*, June 26, 1982.

**28.** Nik Cohn, *Today There Are No Gentlemen* (London: Weidenfeld & Nicholson, 1970).

**29.** Garland, *Heart of Exile.*

**30.** T. R. Fyvel, *The Insecure Offenders* (London: Chatto & Windus, 1961).

**31.** Details from Booker, *Neophiliacs.*

**32.** Mark Abrams, "The Teenage Consumer," LPE Papers 5, *The London Press Exchange,* July 1959.

**33.** Colin MacInnes, *Absolute Beginners* (London: MacGibbon & Kee, 1959).

**34.** Simon Napier-Bell, *You Don't Have to Say You Love Me* (London: Nomis, 1983).

**35.** Richard Dyer, "Don't Look Now: The Male Pin-up," *Screen* 23 (3/4) 1982.

**36.** Back cover blurb, Dave Wallis, *Only Lovers Left Alive,* (London: Blond, 1964). The Rolling Stones were slated to make a movie of this in 1966.

**37.** See T. J. Jackson Lears, "From Salvation to Self-Realization," in Fox and Lears, *Culture of Consumption.*

**38.** Jonathan Miller in the *New Statesman*, 1964, quoted by Dick Hebdige in "In Poor Taste," *Block* 8, 1983.

**39.** Hebdige, *Poor Taste.*

**40.** See Dezo Hoffman's account of the faking of "Beatlemania" in Philip Norman, *Shout!* (London: Elm Tree, 1981), and his own *With the Beatles* (London: Omnibus, 1982).

**41.** See Norman, *Shout!* and Hunter Davies, *The Beatles* (London: Heinemann, 1968).

**42.** Simon Frith and Angela MacRobbie, "Rock and Sexuality," *Screen Education* 24, Winter 1978–79.

**43.** Cohn, *No Gentlemen.*

**44.** Richard Barnes, *Mods!* (London: Eel Pie, 1979).

**45.** *Ibid.*

**46.** Charles Hamblett and Jane Deverson, *Generation X* (London: Tandem, 1964).

**47.** Released in November 1965. See also Dave Marsh, *Before I Get Old: The Story of the Who* (London: Plexus, 1983).

**48.** During 1964, *Billboard* ceased to publish its R&B—black music —charts.

**49.** Abe Peck, *Uncovering the Sixties: The Life and Times of the Underground Press* (New York: Pantheon, 1985).

**50.** Barbara Ehrenreich, *The Hearts of Men* (New York: Anchor/ Doubleday, 1983).

**51.** Peck, *Uncovering*.

**52.** Peter Guralnick's *Sweet Soul Music* (London: Virgin, 1986), gives an exemplary account of the growth and spread of soul music throughout the late fifties and the sixties.

**53.** Ehrenreich, *Hearts*.

**54.** An accessible history of postwar pop can be found in *The Rolling Stone History of Rock 'n' Roll* edited by Jim Miller (New York: Straight Arrow, 1976), which is regularly updated. Lester Bangs' piece on the garage bands from this period, "Proto-Punk," is particularly wonderful.

**55.** Jean Stein and George Plimpton, *Edie* (London: Jonathan Cape, 1982). See also Andy Warhol and Pat Hackett, *Popism: The Warhol 60s* (London: Hutchinson, 1981), and Victor Bockris and Gerard Malanga, *Uptight: The Velvet Underground Story* (London: Omnibus, 1983). Also Jon Savage, "Is This the End?" *Zg 7*, 1982.

**56.** June Singer, *Androgyny* (London: RKP, 1977).

**57.** Booker, *Neophiliacs*, is a one of a kind: a New Right critique of the sixties, heavily laced with Jung and all the detail you could want, from within the period.

**58.** Ehrenreich, *Hearts*.

**59.** Charlie Gillett mentions this process in *Sound of the City*, revised edition (London: Souvenir Press, 1983): "The major American record companies spent a fortune signing up, recording, and publicizing 'the San Franciscan' groups and many more who sounded like them. Although commercially they may only have broken even, they established a once-and-for-all hold on the American record industry, which was not shaken loose in the next fifteen years."

**60.** Ehrenreich, *Hearts*.

**61.** From Frederic Jameson's description of postmodernism,

"Postmodernism and Consumer Society," in Hal Foster, ed., *The Anti-Aesthetic* (San Francisco: Bay Press, 1983).

**62.** EMI Records, U.K., press release, February 1987.

**63.** Paul Ricoeur, "Civilization and National Cultures," in History and Truth (Evanston, Ill.: Northwestern University Press,1965).

**64.** Pat Aufderhide, "The Look of the Sound," in Todd Gitlin, ed., *Watching Television* (New York: Pantheon, 1987).

**65.** Levi's, U.K., press release, Winter 1986.

**66.** In Feburary 1987.

**67.** A phrase from Devo's Gerry Casale, quoted in Michael Shore, *The Rolling Stone Book of Rock Video* (New York: Straight Arrow, 1984).

**68.** Richard Wightman Fox and T. J. Jackson Lears, "Introduction," *Culture of Consumption.*

**69.** Peter Scaping, ed., *BPI Year Book 1986* (London: The British Phonograhic Industry Ltd., May 1986).

**70.** Life-style marketing was an advertising concept that crossed the Atlantic during the sixties: see Kathy Myers, *Understains* (London: Comedia, 1984).

**71.** Susan Sontag, "Notes on Camp," in *A Susan Sontag Reader* (New York: Farrar, Straus and Giroux, 1982).

**72.** Pop (or rock) video became an academic commonplace during 1986 and 1987; one of the best accounts of MTV's "closed loop" is Greil Marcus's "Speaker to Speaker Column," *Artforum*, January 1987.

**73.** For the most accessible account of subcultural theory, see Dick Hebdige, *Subcultures* (London: Methuen, 1979). Also Stuart Hall and Tony Jefferson, eds. *Resistance Through Rituals: Youth Subcultures in Postwar Britain* (London: Hutchinson, 1976).

**74.** Ehrenreich, *Hearts of Men.*

**75.** Rosalind Pollack Petchesky, *Abortion and Women's Choice* (North Eastern Press, 1985).

**76.** *Ibid.*

**McROCK:** Pop as a commodity

**1.** Personal interview with Connie de Nave.

**2.** *Ibid.*

3. Jann Wenner, Introduction to *The Rolling Stone Interviews* (New York: Paperback Library, 1971).
4. Charles Reich, Introduction to Jann Wenner and Charles Reich, *Garcia: A Signpost to New Space* (San Francisco: Straight Arrow Press, 1972).
5. Personal interview with Connie de Nave.
6. David Crosby and Ben Fong Torres, "The David Crosby Interview," reprinted in Wenner, *The Rolling Stone Interviews*.
7. *Ibid*.
8. *Ibid*.
9. Paul Kantner and Grace Slick, "The Jefferson Airplane Interview," reprinted in Wenner, *The Rolling Stone Interviews*.
10. Peter York, *Style Wars* (London: Sidgwick and Jackson, 1980), p. 135.
11. Lisa Robinson, "Eleganza," *Creem*, [April], 1975.
12. Malcolm McLaren interview with Dylan Jones in *i-D*, April 1987, pp. 78–79
13. Dick Hebdige, *Subculture* (London: Methuen, 1979), p. 26.
14. Malcolm McLaren interview.
15. Fred and Judy Vermorel, *The Sex Pistols* (London: Universal/W. H. Allen, 1978), p. 50.
16. *Ibid*.
17. Quoted by Mark Perry in personal interview.
18. Johnny Rotten, *The Guardian*, September 26, 1980.
19. Dave Marsh, *Glory Days* (New York: Pantheon, 1987), p. 208.
20. *Ibid.*, pp. 253–54.

**S I M O N   F R I T H** is director of research at the John Logie Baird Centre, Strathclyde University, Glasgow. He is the author of *Sound Effects* (Pantheon) and a regular contributor to the *Village Voice*.

**S T E V E   P E R R Y** is a contributing editor for *Musician* and for *Rock and Roll Confidential*. He has also written for *Rolling Stone* and the Boston *Phoenix*. He lives in Minneapolis.

**K E N   B A R N E S** is editor of *Radio and Records*, the radio trade magazine. He lives in Los Angeles.

**M A R Y   H A R R O N** is a producer and director for BBC Television. She has contributed to the *Village Voice*, *The Observer*, and *Punk*.

**J O N   S A V A G E** is an editor and contributor for *The Observer* and has also contributed to *The Face* and *The New Statesman*. He is currently writing an account of the Sex Pistols and their impact on English life.